How Much Does a Great School Cost?

How Much Does a Great School Cost?

School Economies and School Values

Barbara J. Smith

ROWMAN & LITTLEFIELD
Lanham • Boulder • New York • London

Published by Rowman & Littlefield
A wholly owned subsidiary of The Rowman & Littlefield Publishing Group, Inc.
4501 Forbes Boulevard, Suite 200, Lanham, Maryland 20706
www.rowman.com

6 Tinworth Street, London SE11 5AL, United Kingdom

Copyright © 2021 by Barbara J. Smith

All rights reserved. No part of this book may be reproduced in any form or by any electronic or mechanical means, including information storage and retrieval systems, without written permission from the publisher, except by a reviewer who may quote passages in a review.

British Library Cataloguing in Publication Information Available

Library of Congress Cataloging-in-Publication Data

Names: Smith, Barbara J., 1956- author.
Title: How much does a great school cost? : school economies and school values / Barbara J. Smith.
Description: Lanham, Maryland : Lexington Books, 2021. | Includes bibliographical references.
Identifiers: LCCN 2020050705 (print) | LCCN 2020050706 (ebook) | ISBN 9781475858884 (cloth) | ISBN 9781475858907 (ebook) | ISBN 9781475858891 (pbk. : alk. paper)
Subjects: LCSH: Education—Finance. | School improvement programs—Finance.
Classification: LCC LB2824 .S65 2021 (print) | LCC LB2824 (ebook) | DDC 371.2/06—dc23
LC record available at https://lccn.loc.gov/2020050705
LC ebook record available at https://lccn.loc.gov/2020050706

∞™ The paper used in this publication meets the minimum requirements of American National Standard for Information Sciences—Permanence of Paper for Printed Library Materials, ANSI/NISO Z39.48-1992.

This work is dedicated to David Booth, who inspired, mentored, and enriched so many possibilities beyond the "red schoolhouse."

Contents

Acknowledgments ix

Introduction 1

PART 1: BUILDING ROADS NOT TAKEN 5

1. Schooling Contexts for Funding 7
2. Defining Greatness, Innovation, and Reform 11
3. Who Minds the Money? 13

PART 2: WHAT'S WORTH CHANGING FOR? 17

4. Social and Emotional Learning 19
5. Global Citizenry and World Languages 25
6. English Language Arts and Fine Arts 29
7. Science and Technology 35
8. Pure Mathematics 41
9. Physical Education 45
10. Classroom Assessment and Standardized Testing 49
11. Reducing Class Size 55
12. Scheduling for Change 59
13. Staffing and Meaningful Roles 65
14. Staff Development 69

15	Learning Facilities	75
16	Being Small	81

PART 3: HOW CAN WE AFFORD CHANGE?   85

17	Inside School Budgets	87
18	Saving Money and Generating Revenue	99

PART 4: PREPARING FOR ANYTHING   105

19	*Imagine If . . .*	107

PART 5: THE CURRENCY OF CHANGE   121

20	To Change or Not to Change . . . That Is the Question . . .	123

Epilogue	131
Appendices	135
References	143
Index	151

Acknowledgments

I asked many people from many varied backgrounds to review many drafts of this book along the way. I owe them a wealth of gratitude for their time and encouragement.

Accomplished children's writer, *Beverley Scudamore*, has a firm spot at the top of my list of acknowledgments. A friend who can accept, inspire, and take weeks to help edit a piece of work, not in her wheelhouse, is worthy of pages of accolades. Her willingness to get inside my reform world, pay attention to the details, and make me dinner after knee replacement surgery was heartfelt and very much appreciated!

David Booth, as the dedication reveals, was my lead mentor. David's insight, courage, and humor kept me on point throughout this project. He will always be a role model for hard work, who with his open spirit saw light-years beyond the norm in schools. The genre of educational reform was never a lonely one, with David in your court. The world lost a piece of kindness when David Booth passed in 2018.

Much appreciated are the words of praise and feedback offered by *Jacqueline Delong*, *Michael Fullan*, *Lisa Gonzales*, *Dennis Kellison*, *Maria Langworthy*, *Doug Reeves*, *Dan Rockwell, and Rick Wormeli*.

After forty years in education, I have drawn on so many key informants along the way. Each of these people made an enduring impact, either through their volunteerism, professionalism, friendship, or a combination thereof: Madelaine Allan, Liz Armitage, Caroline Bernaba, Sharon Bradley, Sam Blyth, Mike Carter, Terence Carter, Tanisha and Richard Chang; Denise Cherry, Bob Chilton, David Chilton, Jim Christopher, Trish Cislak, Luke Coles, Jackie Copp, Stevonna Cordova, Mike Crowley, Clinton Dickens, Teri Domanski, Susan Drake, Lorna Earl, Radu Elias, Don Fawcett, Shannon Foley, Alan Ginsburg, Craig Griffie, Ann Herbert, Ted Herbert, Mhairi

Johnson, Dennis Kellison, Deanna Kensler, Audrey LeVault, Ashley Lopez, Diane Manica, Gillian Martin, Marion McKeiver, Robert McLellan, Jack Miller, Gail Nisbet, Martin Nisbet, Shaune Palmer, Tee Palmer, Martha Perry, Skip Phoenix, Angela Purcell, Dave Quanbeck, Jeremy Rhodes, Val Rixon, Mary Robbins, Ian Robinson, Jalen Rose, Michelle Ruscitti-Miller, Keith Russell, John Scudamore, Anne Shaw, Wayne Somerville, Dave Stevenson, Brian Stone, Tony Upson, Kendall Walton, Kamila Wheeler, Linda Whitfield, William Williams, Anne Wintemute, Martin Wooster, and Tracie Yorke.

My publishing team provided the canvas for helping me share these reform perspectives. To them I owe a gratitude for their trust and dedication to a common interest of further defining greatness in schools, and in this case, affordable ways to get there.

To my husband, Simon, who endured the dozens of *read alouds* of most chapters—thank you for your insight and "economic" food for thought throughout this project. Having worked on a new school project together, after his retirement, we benefitted so much from his business acumen. His willingness to trust my passion, and step into this world of education with authentic humility taught me much about support and leadership.

My daughter, Sarah, is a constant source of inspiration. Having interned in Uganda and South Africa with global nonprofit agencies, she now is completing her MBA at the Ivy School of Business at the University of Western Ontario. She has dedicated much of her work life to supporting young people take trips abroad to volunteer and better understand the global world beyond their current reach. Her drive and persistence are infectious.

My son, Martin, an economics graduate of Carnegie Mellon, taught me much about resilience and having fiercely focused goals. His schooled experiences in Canada, the United States, and Belgium contributed to my constant hope that education can engage boys and young men to meet their potential. Martin's warmth and generous support helped me survive some grueling months of knee replacement rehabilitation.

After all the balancing acts of writing, teaching, mentoring, and making sure our dogs, Mickey, Flossie, and now Blossom were fed, the Smith family survived . . . Mind you, I do regret I had to feed both kids so much fast food, too often in the car on the way to swim and gymnastics practices . . .

Introduction

> Don't tell me what you value, show me your budget, and I'll tell you what you value.—Joe Biden

RESET

If you are serious about improvement in education—hit the "reset" button. Think about what might be affordable outside the realm of how schools spend money today. This book is about looking beyond the main networks of education; it reveals examples of great practices, how much they can cost, and how we can take the remote and move toward more innovative channels in education.

We need to break away from the fixed view that teaching and learning can only happen in a "red schoolhouse." As this read will expose, it takes hard work to implement new ways of doing school; there are simply no short-cuts to building and redesigning great learning institutions.

When the picture on our computer or television screens is not clear, we scramble to push as many buttons as we can to remedy the problem; regrettably, however, when schooling is fuzzy, we rarely change the channel. In a way, the system is caught up in the cycle of "play"; that keeps on doing what's always been done.

Often, the building of a new school is trumpeted as a transforming opportunity, but sadly, these initiatives stop short of innovation. New schools may be larger with renovated lounges, lunchrooms, and lockers, but many fall short of inspiring learning. After an investment of millions of dollars, these schools tend to be no more than cleaner, freshly painted mirrors of existing schools, schools that still look "red."

Rather than view schooling from an outside-in perspective, this book reveals the complexities of addressing the fiscal realities of education from the inside out. This resource features a new multicolored image for schooling, one that doesn't have to color inside the lines. This work has been informed by forty years of teaching experiences in public, independent, charter, international, college preparation, and graduate education programs within single-gender, and co-ed schools that spanned from prekindergarten through twelfth grade.

Rarely do educators and other taxpayers have time to pay attention to, read about, and act on educational economic challenges and possibilities. This resource aims to take the reader on a journey outside the main networks, into the less predictable arenas of the "Netflix" in education. We need to explore new sources to move our compass beyond the limits of schools today. It's time for schools to invest in their off-road tires, and choose new paths that can prepare our students for anything. If we value a different educational outcome for more students, then we need to push for more change.

Education does not have to be on autopilot; we can learn not only how to navigate the remote, but we can redesign it, so we can efficiently improve schools in cost-effective ways. What has emerged from examining educational and business literature is the notion that school values and finances are inheritably linked. Budgets remotely control our schools. Without shifting the budget, we cannot change the educational channel.

Ben Franklin's quote "Drive my business or it will drive thee" is a compelling insight. Is it possible that education could be driving itself, when it continues to perpetuate programs based on the replicated budgets, year after year? This book should be viewed as more than a collection of ideas or a slice in time of a school pricing catalog. While the detailing of how much things cost in schools is necessary when comparing conventional school expenses with funding needed to operate innovative schools, the message that budgets reflect values is central to this discussion. If a school values innovation, then it will need to risk changing how funds are allocated. If schools are expected to embrace change, decision-makers must also be prepared to shift the budget allocation across the board, to reflect new emerging values.

This book addresses the fiscal factor in promoting the design, implementation, and sustainability of schools that go beyond "red." It also introduces the idea of New School, one designed with a new budget framework in mind, one that functions to permit and promote innovation in teaching and learning.

The manuscript follows a path with five stops along the path:

1. Defining greatness
2. Clarifying parameters and conditions for best practices
3. Examining the nature of school budgets

4. Dreaming of a new ideal school
5. Contrasting ideal with traditional schools

The first introductory section, "Building Roads Not Taken," sets the table for greatness by laying out various schooling contexts, terms of reference, and the key players "minding the money." The next section clarifies how existing and new disciplines can emerge in "What's Worth Changing For." Followed by the "what" we need to learn is a close-up view of ideal practices in teaching and learning. The third section "How Can We Afford Change?" features examples of four school budgets that highlight ways in which innovative schools have forged affordable fiscal paths. In the fourth section, "Preparing for Anything," the idea of a New School reveals some possibilities, not yet implemented, as to how we can afford to repurpose schools to address our ongoing quest for greatness.

The final section, *"The Currency of Change,"* and chapter makes a comparison between the costs associated with running the hypothetical New School and a sample conventional school. In this way, the reader can have a glimpse of how many ideas *"worth changing for"* can not only be operationalized, but be affordable. The reader then has a glimpse of how much a great school can cost.

Rather than provide a summary at the end of each chapter, readers are invited to collaborate with other readers by *grappling with ideas*. Such challenges help the reader to rethink, through the lens of a task or question, the potential significance or links to their own experience in education. Such tasks may prove fruitful for professional learning conversations in schools or within undergraduate or graduate course work in education.

This book shares many stories of schooling that are real and worthy of change; at the same time, it highlights glimpses of bold ideas for imagining teaching and learning in a new light. In Linus Pauling's words: "The best way to have a good idea is to have a lot of ideas." This book does not hold back on concrete examples of greatness; if the reader is hungry for fresh ideas, you will be offered ample servings. Be ready for the detailing, but when you reach the threshold of technical examples, adjust your binoculars and simply move on to the next focus of what can be considered greatness in schools. Think about the calls for change, large and small, and what investment of time and money that such improvements might incur.

Finally, pay attention to the idea that values are entrenched, not only in the budget numbers, but in the willingness of decision-makers and implementers to be open to change. Perhaps, talking about a New School, such as the one featured in this book, can lead to the building of more "new" schools, where greatness does not have to be an outlier anymore.

This book was written for all stakeholders who want to rally around school improvement. The public chooses school trustees to be responsible for great schools. School leaders want to inspire students, staff, and families to form great schools. Teachers want to be part of great schools. Non-instructional staff want to contribute to great schools. Parents want to send their children to great schools. University researchers want to inform and be informed by great schools. Students want to have a say in shaping great schools. This text invites all stakeholders to not only celebrate ideas of greatness in schools, but come to understand that innovative and engaging practices can be affordable. These ideas and "grappling" questions can build a rich context for talk about how, and at what cost, we can contribute to building more great schools.

Biden's message that our budgets reflect our values should give some serious pause for thought. It's time to push the reset button!

Part 1

BUILDING ROADS NOT TAKEN

> The tipping point is that magic moment when an idea, trend, or social behavior crosses a threshold, tips, and spreads like wildfire.
>
> —Malcolm Gladwell

BUILDING ROADS NOT TAKEN

What will the tipping point be? The phrase "we do not need to re-invent the wheel" is often echoed by forces that preserve the status quo. The notion of innovation fitting into an existing budget means that new ideas must compete with older ways of doing school. For fresh ideas to take shape, we must embrace the idea of a new wheel and a new path down a road not taken.

Such a path can be risky for the status funding quo. The autopsies of the "walking dead" reforms in education reveal much about good plans, that were poorly implemented, or naive plans void of big picture alignment.

This first section introduces varied school contexts, how a working definition of greatness in schools evolved, and a summary of the players who make key financial decisions in schools. Gladwell suggests that we need a wildfire of the education sort, and when we become more aware of what's worth changing for, we can move beyond the tipping point, so that quality schooling for all can be the norm.

Chapter 1

Schooling Contexts for Funding

Different kinds of schools have distinct expenses and revenues. Public schools, charter schools, independent/international schools, and private schools have specific structures that guide how monies are spent in these distinct schools.

PUBLIC SCHOOLS

Typically, public schools break up the expenditure pie with salaries leading the way. However, it is difficult to unpack individual public school budgets, as they are intertwined with a central budget that supports multiple schools at the same time. Many schools in North America require significant renovations to their physical plants, and so school boards wind up making decisions about modernizing and increasing the size of schools at the same time as closing smaller ones. The premise that maintaining fewer schools will reduce the overall costs tends to fuel such arguments. The costs of central office infrastructure to support individual schools, however, are not widely publicized, but studies addressing the necessity for such roles and services would be of interest to many.

CHARTER SCHOOLS

Salaries in charter schools do vary, but there tends to be added expenses for noninstructional staff. If a charter school is linked to a central office within the public or charter system, then some administrative expenses are absorbed for multiple schools, public/charter at the same time, thus reducing the need for accounting teams in each school. There are other charters, however, that operate as a self-contained unit, therefore, requiring additional staff, to ensure financial accountability. In some cases, charter schools outsource their payroll, and human relations to consulting firms. Many charter schools also incur a significant financial burden when faced with the purchase or leasing of facilities.

INDEPENDENT/INTERNATIONAL SCHOOLS

Like some charter schools, independent or international schools are organized as separate operations, requiring people to manage the business and finances associated with the school. Different from public schools that are funded from taxes, independent and international schools rely mainly on revenues from tuition. The salaries vary from school to school, but most tend to be at or within reach of the public school salaries in the region. These schools tend to have property and facilities that are maintained through capital fundraising supported by the alumni. A Board of Trustees or Governors provides oversight over the independent and international schools, so that all profits go back into the school.

PRIVATE SCHOOLS

While private schools also charge tuition, they do not have boards and there is no requirement that profits go back into the school. The owner(s) of the school determine how funds are distributed. The physical plants of private schools can vary, from renovated schools, to storefront offices, to church basements. They tend to be smaller schools with tuition as the major source of funding. Tutoring businesses operate much like private schools, except that the physical plants may be individual homes or students may sign up for support at a central location.

Further detailing of actual budgets will be the focus of future chapters. While this oversight provides a summary of key expenses and revenues, attention to specific line items in budgets reveal more about the similarities and distinctiveness of budgets within different kinds of schools.

As much as the costs for schooling can vary within and across institutions, so too, can the definition of greatness shift from school to school. Before responding to the question, *how much does a great school cost?* It is important to define what is meant by "greatness" in the context of this inquiry. The next chapter unpacks the term from a variety of perspectives.

Grappling with Ideas

- What kinds of school funding oversight are you familiar with?
- What kinds of revenues might be generated in a school setting?
- What are some initial questions you are grappling with after reading these first introductory chapters?

Chapter 2

Defining Greatness, Innovation, and Reform

We do not need to be bystanders in discussions that define greatness in schools. Imagine if schools paid more attention to voices from the inside. Imagine what schools could be like if survey feedback was gathered from parents, students, and staff on an annual basis. Schools are complex and, as such, cannot be simplified as derivatives of statistical analysis. To address quality in schools, we must embrace qualitative data; as well, we need to view trends and patterns in quantitative data. A blend of educational literature and quantitative and qualitative data from a small sampling of professional voices can help us reimagine ideas for school improvement and ways to save money to fund such changes.

Part of this project involved the collection of responses from sixteen international educators. Their responses acknowledged the complexities of a classroom context, aware that quantitative measures cannot capture all that is great in schools. Many respondents held complex views of greatness in schools; they did not share the same textbook answers, their views revealed a rich assortment of passionate and eclectic values. It was surprising the word "innovation" was only referenced once, and the word "reform" was absent entirely. However, after careful review of all their responses, the notion of *greatness in schools,* according to this small sampling, was synthesized and defined for this examination as "inspired learning through responsible actions in an inclusive culture." Without having a common understanding of what it means to be a great school, it is a challenge to guide innovation and reform efforts.

While this book does not profess to claim an absolute definition for greatness, I would say that this collective perspective would align well with research-supported studies and accounts of deep learning. It seems logical that inspired learning through responsible actions in inclusive cultures would require stakeholders to embrace innovation and reform. While many innovations may not pass the test of time, or in too many cases, not provided enough time, they remain evidence of reform. Innovation and reform remain at the mercy of implementation. We do not innovate or seek reform in schools for the sake of change; rather, it is the goal of seeking greatness in schools that requires a need for change. To innovate and reform means that every aspect of a school can be privy to positive change, in effect *no improvement left behind*.

For many educators, the mere mention of reform is often met with a sigh, not of relief, but of frustration. In a way, it's ironic that such responses are the antithesis of the goal of engagement, but for many, the piling on of reform after reform has led to mistrust and disillusionment. Cries of "Here we go again" sound off through the halls, staff rooms, and parking lots of schools full of improvement promise.

While this book attempts to capture snapshots of greatness in schools in the moment, it also aims to inspire readers to engage in further innovative and reforming action. As new schools form and transform, we will further define greatness, and as such, we will graze more on outlier positions. To plan and implement for such change, we will need to come to understand alternative or expanded visions for funding schools. Determining who minds the money in schools, and understanding how these key people embrace change, or not, can influence whether a school can implement practices that lead to greatness.

Grappling with Ideas

- What references to greatness in schools were a surprise for you?
- How do the words "innovate" and "reform" resonate for you?
- What ideas linked with your perspective on school greatness?
- What questions remain with respect to other ideas about school greatness?

Chapter 3

Who Minds the Money?

Building great schools cannot happen in a vacuum. Funds are required to navigate the change; people who mind the money are critical to the reform process. There is no need to be shy about the handlers responsible for minding and distributing school dollars. Schooling of any kind is an expensive, but necessary, part of a civilized society. All schools do not need to operate and implement curriculum in the same way. This message, to those who "mind" the money, is a critical point. These key people in schools and school districts are responsible for ensuring that funds are in the bank to pay teachers and support staff. How well money managers are willing to deviate from existing patterns represents the opportunity, or not, for innovation.

There can be many money managers in school: superintendents, executive directors, accountants in a school or Head Office, outsourced consultants, trustees, representatives of teacher unions, student government or parent associations, principals, and teachers. What kinds of funds each stakeholder may manage can vary?

TEACHERS AS SUBSTANTIAL FORCE

A considerable piece of the funding pie goes directly to paying salaries, and many teachers, with collective bargaining agreements, some better than others, have considerable control over public funds. Many public pay scales can set the tone for the kind of pay offered to independent, private, and charter school teachers, who may be operating with contracts developed independently of teacher unions. Teachers, and those who negotiate contracts, therefore, mine and mind a significant proportion of a school's budget.

The idea of a pay grid, while common in typical public schools, is not as common in charter, independent or private schools. Pay equity can often lack transparency. Some schools that pay teachers far less than their "public" school counterparts can have more turnover, and it could be argued, that such schools with "revolving" doors, lack the consistency and talent to support a great school.

Teacher input into what constitutes school greatness can be limited to the lens of contractual agreements, often assuming—"what's good for teachers is good for students." When it comes to how schools are organized and what to teach, many teachers have less say in the public system. The accountability movement could be viewed as a force, castrating teachers by the unwavering drive for "sameness."

NON-INSTRUCTIONAL STAFF AS SERVICE PROVIDERS

Non-instructional staff play a significant role in schools, as well as in the district central offices. Depending on the position, these individuals may engage in direct or indirect roles, in terms of allocating school funding. The front office staff, the maintenance team, and in some schools, the security and business staff form a base of support for the teachers and administrators in a school. The number of staff positions in a public system is usually determined by a staffing formula based on the number of students enrolled in a school. In public systems, support staff fall under contractual agreements that tend to be negotiated, as well. In charter, independent, or international schools, the pay and number of support positions and services can vary.

And what are the costs of managing the money? At one end of the spectrum, I've seen extensive finance departments in public school settings with significant funding set aside to support the human capital that minds the budget for the entire school district. At the other end of the spectrum, I've witnessed a volunteer Board Chair for a charter school write a payroll check by hand. The costs of money managers can vary from school to school.

SCHOOL LEADERS AS MESSENGERS AND MONITORS

In public schools, the principal tends to be in a messenger and monitoring role. This school leader rarely handles much money or has much input into how it is distributed; rather, the central office provides fiscal oversight. The notion that budgets are allocated from above, is one way of managing a school, but being responsible for generating a budget at the school level is something that happens more in charter and independent schools.

UNIVERSITY AND OTHER EXPERT INFLUENCERS

University professors can and should inform and influence school leaders. Being separate from the day-to-day operations and finances of a school can keep such players away from the fiscal reality of schools, yet understanding how schools can be innovative does require consultants to comprehend fully the costs associated, not only with specific advances, but how a shifting in funding focus can affect the overall school operations. Such accounts of schools should contribute to the body of educational literature, and at the same time, provide cases for school leadership and graduate courses.

SCHOOL TRUSTEES

School trustees are elected officials who represent the school community; at the same time they provide legal oversight for the institution. They are officials who need to be aware of what happens in the schools they govern. A clearly defined chain of command is usually comprised of trustees at the top of the food chain, in a public or nonprofit school entity. It is often recommended that trustees be hands off the operation of a school.

Trustees of independent schools and charter schools tend to serve smaller populations of students. At one school, the business director worked closely with the school principal to prepare the budget that was presented to the board annually. The board also had a finance committee that provided further oversight for the school. Early on, we learned that new programming meant changes to the budget. In other words, money just didn't appear out of thin air; it needed to come from an existing program.

To keep costs down in one school, we hired a teaching principal, and took extra time to reduce unnecessary spending. Trustees are responsible for providing oversight over the operational leader in the school, in addition to passing the school budget and coordinating the annual audit for the school, trustees hire the leader, assess the leader and are responsible for planning for leadership succession. In private schools, there are no trustees. In such cases, the owner takes full responsibility for the school and its profits. Trustees, and/or school owner play an important role in minding the finances of the school.

PARENTS AS TAXPAYERS OR TUITION SOURCES

Parents, as card-carrying taxpayers, may have strong beliefs about the way schools spend money. Their voices tend to be routed through school trustees. It is common for families to get involved in fundraising projects to support new technology, or other teaching and learning initiatives, but rarely do they view the breakdown of operational costs at the school or district level. Parents of students in charter schools can have opportunities for a closer view at school budgets, but usually this happens when parents sit on finance committees or hold a trustee position.

Some parents have challenged the spending choices in schools. And more recently, students have stepped up to have any say in their education. On March 24, 2018, families joined forces to take part in the *March of Our Lives*, not only in Washington, DC, but in over 800 other cities in the United States and around the world:

> The event followed the Stoneman Douglas High School shooting. . . . Protesters <wanted> universal background checks on all gun sales, raising the federal age of gun ownership and possession to the age of 21. . . and a ban on the sale of high-capacity magazines in the United States. Turnout was estimated to be between 1.2 to 2 million people in the United States, making it one of the largest protests in American history.[1]

A great school must be a safe school, and better conditions require funding, either from additional sources, or an alteration of existing budgets.

It seems ironic that student voices tend to be absent at decision-making tables, nor represented in panels at conferences about how to improve the state of schooling. Social media has given young people some tools to respond. Their voices should not be muted, nor should they be omitted; they are major players in the learning community and have greater stakes in the future.

Grappling with Ideas

- What access do you have to a school budget?
- How difficult is it to access new funds for an innovative program?
- What ways can school reduce current operational costs?

NOTE

1. en.wikipedia.org/wiki/Student activism.

Part 2

WHAT'S WORTH CHANGING FOR?

> We do kind of need to blow up the system and start fresh . . . Well, maybe not blow up the whole thing, but at least some corners.
>
> —David Perkins

WHAT'S WORTH CHANGING FOR?

Engaging curriculum and quality programming in schools should be at the heart of learning in a changing world. If we need, as Perkins suggests, to blow up the system and start fresh, then we need to determine what's worth learning and what conditions can foster best practices to get there. What are some new or transformed pedagogies and what conventional disciplines are essential? How can disciplines be organized so that time is afforded for deep learning within and outside the classroom context? The first part of this section deals with an examination of change in six key areas of study.

Change can also serve as the catalyst for improvement in instructional conditions. The later part of this section addresses instructional conditions for change. Hargreaves and Fullan (1996) suggested that schools are worth fighting for to lessen the burden of overload placed on educators expected to implement failed reforms. Nowadays, it seems like every penny is worth fighting for.

Chapter 4

Social and Emotional Learning

Often touted as central to learning, social and emotional learning (SEL) courses lack the status of mainstream disciplines. It was no accident that SEL has been placed first in the list of essential school disciplines. There is a need for this subject matter to be much more than a checklist of learning habits or effort scores. We can learn about many different subjects in school, but without physical and mental health, young people are limited in terms of doing anything with such knowledge.

Beyond the "All about Me" unit in primary school, there are extensive themes and life lessons that students can learn in deliberate and meaningful ways. It can be argued that each distinct form of intelligence contributes to the overall "whole" of one's intelligence. By minimizing the importance of SEL, the school, in effect, can contribute to diminishing their students' overall intellectual return. Schools that explicitly teach courses in SEL see the value of all intelligences, and thus are better prepared and capable of reducing learning gaps among students.

Life skills, character building, health education, guidance, and leadership courses have the potential for promoting positive mental health. The costs of mental illness in many communities have skyrocketed in the past few decades; schools need to teach proactive ways of building self-esteem, empathy, and resilience. Sobering statistics include the following:

- Incidence of a major depressive event in teenagers rose by 37% between 2005 and 2014 (Mojtabai, Olfson, & Han, 2016).
- Suicide rate in the United States increased 24% between 1999 and 2014 (Curtin, Warner, & Hedegaard, 2016).

We need to make more room in the curriculum for mental health, if only to address the compelling data of increased depression and suicide rates.

Research has revealed much about the conditions that limit SEL. Often schools will develop or adopt programs to help students address underage alcohol and drug use, eating disorders, and a full range of poor health-related choices that include bullying and cyberbullying behavior. While the separating out of relevant issues from the health education curriculum is a popular response, it nevertheless can lead to short-lived solutions when the focus is on "illness" prevention. Strong health education programs, developed with a proactive emphasis on positive pro-social and personal skills, should have issues of bullying embedded within the curriculum, rather than have individual issues become the focus of crisis management. The U.S. Department of Health and Human Services identified loneliness as part of a list of risk factors that lead to premature mortality. What are the concrete actions happening in schools that address loneliness? How is reducing loneliness a deliberate part of school curriculum? It's not enough to feel empathetic for a short burst of attention to a literary character in English Language Arts (ELA). A sense of belonging is an important cultural feature of a great school. SEL programs need to be developed and updated, and not be placed on the back burner of a school schedule.

LANGUAGE ARTS AS INTEGRATED MEDIUM FOR SEL

SEL curriculum can also be aligned with ELA expectations. Given the emphasis on encouraging the reading, writing, and talking about social justice issues, a carefully designed character, leadership, or service-learning class can augment ELA learning outcomes. According to Brooks (2017): "Through service-learning, students can gain significant experiences of reflecting and acting upon the world alongside fellow students, faculty, and community partners" (p. 7). In one secondary charter school, we coordinated a weekly student field trip to a government-supported nursing home which housed over a thousand seniors. Students formed relationships with a senior who, in return, helped them with goal setting activities. Each week the students interviewed their buddy and used the information in their English class to write and publish an anthology of senior biographies.

In a writing workshop in an elementary charter school in Virginia, students were encouraged to view video accounts of CNN's *Tribute to Heroes*. They were given the option of sending in their votes for nominees. This activity led to searching the web for meaningful charities. The students drafted, edited, and mailed letters to the President of the United States asking for support of a cause they wanted to promote. In one letter, one student asked the government to provide more funds for improved juvenile brain cancer drugs. Many students received responses from President Obama, adding to the authenticity of the task. In one case, after decades of zero funding for juvenile cancer drugs, a bill was passed that year to begin further funding in this area.

A SOCIAL AND EMOTIONAL CLASS ON ITS OWN

Schools can offer proactive opportunities to build resilience, kindness, and the capacity to work well with others. A SEL class can create authentic space for planning and implementing service-learning projects in school, communities, or global arenas. The linking of SEL with Health education makes good sense as mental health is at the core of all health habits and choices. Depending on the school, an SEL course can also be a space for housing religious studies.

An SEL course can breathe life into a school mission, and support positive school behaviors. A well-placed and coordinated SEL curriculum can decrease the time administrators need to be involved in disciplinary duties. SEL courses can also integrate current events, metacognition (reflecting on how we learn), yoga, meditation, career preparation, and goal setting. According to an analysis of fifteen peer-reviewed studies by the *Educational Psychology Review*, school-based meditation practices had a range of benefits including kids reporting fewer feelings of anxiety and stronger friendships; teachers noted that meditation led to more settled classrooms. At the high school level, the need to build in themes of resilience, adaptation, and employability skills, as well as exposure to disciplines, such as psychology and sociology, can increase the depth and breadth of a SEL course offer.

Internships into the world of work should not be an option for students; expanding a social and emotional course to include career education can be a powerful authentic part of a school curriculum. Technology Education teacher Craig Griffie (2018), from the *Brown Deer Schools* noted: "Students show up early to school and I run them through the Apprentice-level curriculum provided by the Carpenter's Union. If students complete the course, they are guaranteed carpenter apprenticeships and given 500 hours of credit." College admissions and many places of employment pay attention to self-less activity.

Most service-learning opportunities have built-in leadership experiences. Featured in the United States and Canada, *Habitat for Humanity* (habitat.org) gives young people an opportunity to build homes for needy families and *Round Square* (roundsquare.org) reaches a more global network. *Round Square* currently operates in fifty countries and is built around six ideals: Internationalism, Democracy, Environmentalism, Adventure Leadership, and Service. The *4-H Club* offers many leadership opportunities for young people. In addition to a full range of STEM programming, 4-H offers an impressive civic engagement program where the development of lifeskills supports "help grow 4-H youth into true leaders" (https://4-h.org/parents/programs-at-a-glance/). In Canada, *Outward Bound* (outwardbound.ca), the *Duke of Edinburgh Awards* (dukeofed.org) and more recently, the *Canada Service Corps* (canada.ca/en/employment-social-development/services/canada-service-corps.html) offer key incentives that encourage young people to help others. Encouraging students and staff to consider the possibilities of linking with local, national, or international agencies can be a worthwhile investment.

There is no doubt that character education has a significant place in great schools. According to Newton (2017), "Children spend nearly as much of their waking lives in school as they do at home. Their character development cannot be seen solely as the responsibility of parents and careers" (p. 2). He added: "Gone are those back rows of passive, robotic students who will do just enough to keep off your radar . . . character education is something every school should recognise they need to do purposefully" (p. 3). Rather than relying on teaching about personal and social growth in a random, responsive or reactive manner, a comprehensive curriculum can be proactive by synthesizing deliberate habits in a coordinated way. At one charter school, we developed the following ten course program, broken down by grade, as well as character education, school service, community service, global service, and health education. See sample in Table 4.1.

Rather than touch on themes for only a month, we chose to have one grade be the ambassadors of a value or behavior for the whole school. Classes that emphasize SEL may be taught by homeroom teachers, advisory mentors, guidance counselors, school nurses, librarians, special education teachers, technology coordinators, assistant principals, or the school principal. Such courses do not require a teacher to have a clinical psychology degree or a Masters of Social Work.

The costs associated with offering SEL programming in schools can be well worth the investment in time and money. Schools may need to revise current job descriptions; in some cases, teachers already assigned to homeroom or advisory groups could take on the deliberate teaching of a SEL course. In other cases, additional staffing might be required; budgeting for additional staff roles to teach SEL classes could range between $35,000 and $75,000.

Resources to support coursework could range from $50 to $100 per student, depending on the need for supplementary materials. Some schools may purchase books to augment a customized program. The field trip costs of transporting students to visit local senior homes or participate in community service programs could add upwards of $1000 to $5000 to a school budget,

Table 4.1 Sample SEL Curriculum Outline

Grade	Character Education	School Service	Community Service	Global Service	Health Education
PK	Be Caring	Black Tie Event	Humane Society	World Wildlife Federation	Senses; Clean Hands
K	Be Kind	Gold Ribbon Day (PK Fashion Show)	Planting Trees	We Walk for Water (We.org)	Healthy Snacks; Road/car safety
1	Be a Friend	Grandparent's Day	Children's Hospital	International Pen Pals	Water Safety
2	Be Courteous	Turkey Dinner Donation	Books for America	Mosquito Nets for Africa (kiva.org)	Healthy Eyes and Ears; Healthy Meals
3	Be a Good Sport	Staff Talent Show	St. Jude's Trikathon	Right to Play	Smoke-free Spaces; First Aid
4	Be Brave	Purple Ribbon Day (Founder's Birthday)	Anti-Smoking Campaign	The Zambia Project	Nutrition
5	Be a Citizen	Can and Coat Drive	Community Clean Up	Earth Day	Internet Safety; Hygiene
6	Be a Team Player	United Nations International Day	PowerPoint Competition	Save the Children	Puberty; Eating Disorders
7	Be Responsible	Field Day	St. Jude's Mathathon	Amnesty International	Family Life Education; CPR
8	Be a Leader	Do something.org	Walk for the Homeless	International Disaster Relief	Drug Education; Avoiding Infection

depending on the frequency of visits. Sustaining a vigorous SEL program for a 300-student school might amount to $25,000. The costs to society of not offering such programs could be much more. If schools values social and emotional and emotional learning, they will need to fund it one way or another.

Grappling with Ideas

- How do your teachers gather evidence of personal and social learning?
- Discuss the advantages and disadvantages of merging character education, service learning, and health education.
- How can the school schedule limit or support the teaching of personal and social learning?

Chapter 5

Global Citizenry and World Languages

The vast scope of content in History and Geography makes it a challenge sometimes, for the notion of civics via local to global citizenship, to hold a substantial place within the traditional boundaries of a Social Studies program. In many ways, the notion of being a good citizen holds value because it adds a sense of purpose to knowing about the world, past and present, far and wide. While the study of civics, law and world religions can fall within the realm of Social Studies, the idea of housing citizenship with community and global service can also fit within the discipline domain of social and emotional learning.

So much attention in Social Studies courses is focused on memorizing facts about the state, province or country, but it is important to think about how we all interrelate on this planet. Many educators are inspired by innovative programs aimed at global citizenry. Responding to the need to develop programs to support refugees, Mia Eskelund and Polly Akhurst co-founded the *Sky School* that sponsors social entrepreneurship courses globally.

UN simulation games can be very effective at helping young people come to understand different perspectives. According to Patti (2018) students use card prompts and scenarios "to start conversations around tough challenges with the aim of inventing solutions that benefit everyone." The simulation tool was taken to Tonga to help the government build a strategy for the future: "Around 100 ordinary citizens were given scenarios, such as the future of the country's water system, and then asked to rearrange cards to guide discussions and find solutions" (Patti, 2018).

The *Model United Nations* program offers rich opportunities for students to simulate how varied countries around the world come together to address global issues at the UN. The program encourages students to confront issues from the perspective of representing an assigned country. Students "develop an appreciation of differing viewpoints, experience the challenges of negotiation, see the rewards of cooperation, broaden their world view, and discover the human side of international relations and diplomacy."[1]

At the International School of Brussels, all Middle School students took part in Model UN, as a mandatory part of their Social Studies program. Unfortunately, such experiences tend to be optional in schools, that is, organized as after school or club activities. In these times, when people have questions about the acceptance of refugees and immigrants, such activities can be very helpful in developing further empathy and understanding. The cost for forty students to participate and attend a Model UN program at the national level (meals included) is approximately $10,000 plus additional funding for transportation. The cost of hosting a MUN event at your own school is probably less than $250.

Students at younger ages can be involved in connecting with other cultures around the world, too. The *Flat Stanley* stories present a wonderful opportunity for making global connections. After reading one or more in the series, students can take pictures with a Flat Stanley image at different places in their community, and then mail them to students at other places around the world. He may be sitting on the Liberty Bell in Philadelphia in one photograph and in another, taking a ride on the London Eye. When students open their envelope full of images and stories of Stanley's travels, this can prompt an appreciation and curiosity for cultures around the world.

WORLD LANGUAGES

Understanding and being able to use other languages help us appreciate other cultures. As the world becomes a place that can appreciate one another more, learning about World Languages makes increasingly good sense. While not all learners of additional languages may become bilingual, it is possible to learn to understand one another, and in such circumstances come to appreciate each other's cultures.

In addition to hiring World Language teachers, schools may also access online programs at a cost of approximately $100 per student. For each additional language, such costs would double. While many promoters of commercial products may place significant value on the streamlining of a common approach to teaching second language acquisition from year to year, it may not be necessary to over-invest in complete programs. Schools may use parts of kits and use more economical software programs to augment how the teacher coordinates the curriculum based on the state or provincial guidelines. It is fitting to speak of World Languages as a distinct language acquisition subject; but also, as a liberal art, it can also connect with Social Studies.

Finally, budgeting for field trips that bring History and Geography to life, are essential for cultivating global citizenry. Over and above learning new languages or participating in a *Model UN* experience, a healthy field trip budget for a school Social Studies program might cost between $45,000 and $60,000 for a small school of 300, without asking families to subsidize such experiences.

Following the description of global citizenry, it makes sense to address global cultures in relation to the languages that define them. The costs of supporting ideal global citizenry programming (Social Studies and World Languages) in schools can range between $100,000 to $300,000 depending on the need and dependency on others to develop lessons and materials.

Grappling with Ideas

- Discuss your experiences in Social Studies.
- Why is it necessary for Social Studies to address local and global issues?
- Discuss how volunteering abroad supports global citizenry.
- How can World Language courses support global citizenry?

NOTE

1. nmun.org.

Chapter 6

English Language Arts and Fine Arts

This grouping of English Language Arts (ELA) and Fine Arts seemed to fall together quite naturally. While they can be linked in project-based learning activities, there are fundamental aspects of each discipline that can benefit from the concentrated study of each discipline.

ELA tends to be funded much more than Fine Arts in schools. The dedicated time afforded to daily instruction of ELA far outweighs the time designated for Music, Visual Arts, Drama, Dance, and other more technical art forms. There tends to be more ELA teachers in schools, which accounts for the significant human capital costs and status of this mainstream discipline.

Fewer arts teachers are hired to teach arts classes that are featured less often in the weekly elementary school schedule; arts at the high school level are typically optional or elective courses. To make room in the curriculum for arts courses, time needs to be carved out of the existing school day. It makes sense that a reduction in ELA time at the elementary level would enable new disciplines to emerge, or subjects, with less status, such as fine arts, to expand and be part of a regular compulsory school experience.

ENGLISH LANGUAGE ARTS

It is a tall order to coordinate all the moving parts of a quality ELA program. What are the most effective and engaging ways for students to master reading, writing, speaking, listening and media literacy? Applying best practices in each of these areas of ELA requires ongoing funding.

Many educators consider reading a subject area of its own. With increased emphasis on differentiation, the textbook industry has generated close to thirty levels of reading materials, mainly emphasizing comprehension and fluency. The time required for teachers to move students through the alphabet of difficulty levels is extensive, so much so that reading, in elementary schools, can often be viewed as the curriculum, and everything else, unfortunately, a few appetizers on the side. Re-thinking how such resources are used or whether the purchase of such alphabet bundles of materials is necessary, could lead to savings in time and money. Educators need time to build a fluid ELA curriculum that would reduce the reliance on commercial products as drivers. Such reform could lead to a possible two-thirds reduction of material costs, reduced overlap of expectations, and more opportunity for reading choice.

Fictional reading materials for primary and junior level students in a small school can cost approximately $3000 for forty students. Novels, plays, and poetry anthologies for middle school programming (Grades 6–10) can cost upwards of $6,000 and Senior High, an additional $3000. Often schools keep many of the reading materials and re-use them in future years. Other costs associated with reading, writing, speaking, and media literacy include the purchase of specific software. After experiencing firsthand how much Flocabulary engages students, it is well worth the school fee of $2,000 per year. Access to *Flocabulary*, can provide students and teachers with enjoyable raps that support key concepts in multiple areas of ELA. Students can also generate their own raps using multimedia technology.

Costs for some digital resources can vary, but a safe estimate for budgeting for such digital resources for a small school of 160 might add up to approximately $8000. While classroom libraries should have ample access to dictionaries, thesauruses, and rhyming dictionaries, students should also have their own designated reference tools for use at school. While such costs would not be repeated each year, it is estimated in 2018, that a school of 160 would need approximately $1,350 <based on $300 (picture dictionaries K-grades 2) + $150 (dictionary grades 3–5) + $300 (dictionary 6–12) + $300 (thesaurus grades 3–5) + $300 (thesaurus grades 6–12)>.

Having access to current events in the form of print newspapers and magazines for younger students and digital access for older students can augment and link social justice messages to what is happening in the world around them. The anticipated costs for print and digital news/magazines subscriptions could cost as much as $1500/year, depending on the number of resources needed to support the curriculum.

While we encourage students to read fiction, and more nonfiction, we often fail to guide our students toward reading their own writing, something that would be worthy for many readers to read, beyond the teacher. Learning how to write in response to reading is not enough. For students to be prepared for college and life, they need to learn how to write friendly and business letters, poetry, arguments, research and reports. E-pal programs, for instance, give students a real audience for writing and reading, and rarely cost much to introduce in classes.

Future novelists also need a forum for writing many different fictional genres. A solid curriculum will have a progressive introduction each year of a focus on reading and writing different genres. Students need more time to grapple with reading and writing drama, adventure, humor, social justice, fantasy, and science fiction. A rich writing program will also feature both digital and written forms of work. Each classroom should have printers so young writers can print off drafts and make handwritten edits, and older students, who have mastered the art of track changes, can view their draft, final, and published work. The costs of providing printers for fourteen classrooms can be approximately $6000. Students can also begin working on their own novels and poetry anthologies, spend upwards of two to three years completing long-term projects. The costs for printing novels for a class of twenty students can cost between $350 and $400. An emphasis on communications and media literacy is critical to shaping greatness in ELA programming.

Teachers and students can be more engaged in ELA classrooms when they are participating in meaningful activities. How often do all students write speeches to run for school president? How often do all students learn the art of debate, not just the few who show up after school for debate club? How often do students write and respond to a series of correspondences to soldiers or diplomats abroad, not simply one letter? How often do students develop their own rating scales for colleges? How often do students write and publish their own autobiographies or stories about the lives of others? How often are students permitted to write with others? How often do students publish research? How often do students have a chance to write their own novels? How often do all students plan for and implement lessons to teach each other? How often do students have a chance to create their own Dewey Decimal System, make plans for a book store, or re-design the school library? When there are more of these kinds of memories, and fewer experiences of answering questions after each chapter, than more ELA classes will be well on their way to being exceptional.

So where does a teacher go to begin thinking differently about how to increase student engagement in ELA classes? Apart from attending, and ideally, someday presenting at ELA-focused conferences, the list of inspiring websites for engaging students in ELA classes is endless. A popular membership for ELA professionals includes the National Council for Teachers of English (NCTE) which offers a full assortment of quality resources, particularly through its "readwritethink" website (http://www.readwritethink.org).

Greatness in an ELA class is not reading a dozen novels in one year or circling the correct comprehension answer on a multiple-choice test. Rather, it is more about facilitating for all students—memorable experiences that matter.

I often wonder why, if teachers value books so much, and want students to value books so much, that we do not have more teachers and students writing books? Finding out what sticks by surveying students can be helpful.

FINE ARTS

Using the Fine Arts to support and engage students in ELA and other subject areas is often a special glue used by many exceptional teachers. While the integration of Fine Arts as a medium for expressing learning makes good sense, it is imperative that space be carved out for the development of the arts on their own, as well. As documented in much research, the Fine Arts have a significant role to play in learning. Fine Arts can include Music, Visual Arts, Dramatic Arts, Graphic Arts, Dance, and a full range of more current technological arts.

Music education tends to have a strong following in many schools, although access to qualified Music teachers can vary from school to school. The research that addresses the relationship between increased Math understanding and musical talent contributes to added interest in this specific art form. Many elementary schools feature choral Music, but some also include instrumental Music beginning as early as third grade. Recorder, guitar, or drum programs are popular, and often the costs of instruments are subsidized by families renting from local music stores. Quality Music programs require stereo systems, access to music, sheet music, and technology equipment for recording music generated by and performed by the students. It is costly to outfit a new school with the materials needed to implement a comprehensive Music program. Expenses for maintaining a quality program could add up to approximately $10,000 for Grades 6–12 instrument rentals with an additional $1,500 for sheet music, and other production-related materials. Materials for students in PK to Grade 5 classes could cost approximately $3,000 to maintain drums, recorders, and various percussion instruments, in addition to costs associated with access to existing music.

Visual Arts programming should be much more than offering a "craft-making" experience. Most school districts offer specific guidelines for giving students an arts apprenticeship-type experience. Schools aim to hire educators who are adept at using multiple mediums. Outfitting a great Visual Arts class involves stocking shelves with many materials including assorted paper, canvas, portfolios, sketching pads, paint, charcoal, pastels, molding clay, paint brushes, and cleaning products. The cost of maintaining a kiln, as well as the technology for graphic artwork also needs to be added to the bottom line cost for quality Fine Arts programming. To showcase student, teacher, and community art work, it is important to build in programming and funding for art exhibitions. Rather than exposing students to all kinds of art forms in a random way, a quality program would determine different areas of concentration each year. Not only would such an emphasis provide more time for students to move beyond being novice artists, the overall costs for the entire program would be less. In other words, students do not need to make and bake sculptures every year. It is anticipated that estimated costs for a quality Visual Arts program might be approximately $10,000 for a small K-12 school with 160 students.

While Dramatic Arts can be integrated to a degree within a subject matter as an activity, it should also be considered a discipline on its own, linked to the context of drama, that being, in a stage play, within television programming, and within film or online media work. Being exposed to the genre of playwrights should be more than a traditional nod and trudging through Shakespeare. Shorter scripts and plays can invite reading and interactive participation and the learning of what actions, beyond words, can add to a story. Drama can be a key force in developing communication skills, and as such, funding for costuming, makeup, and props need to be included in school budgets. With access to more YouTube and internal online school portals, the costs of video production can be significantly reduced. Video cameras, used in multiple subject areas, would augment a quality drama program, as well. Schools need to factor in costs for lighting and stage rentals. It is difficult to determine what it costs to facilitate Drama as a subject on its own, or as part of an ELA program, but a generous estimate might $5,000, plus or minus $1,000 depending on the needs of single or multiple productions is a good starting point.

Photography, film, television, and other Media Arts are powerful art forms that tend to be less accessible for all students. Such courses are often offered as electives, reducing the value of such twenty-first-century skills to more auxiliary status in schools. More progressive arts curricula should equip students with the skills and understandings to create videos, films, and websites to convey ideas. The costs of maintaining various cameras and computers, as well as the printing costs for photography exhibitions might be estimated at approximately $2,500.

Dance can also be a specific area of study, but it is often integrated with Physical Education programs. It can be part of more wide-scale dramatic productions on stage or in film, television, or other technological media. Dance can add much to a dramatic or musical production, live or in other media forms. Some teachers may invite students to express their understandings using dance. Quality dance programs require access to a variety of music, quality speakers, ballet bars and a room with at least one mirrored wall. As well, students may require dance attire or specialized shoes. It is estimated that budgeting for an annual Dance program might be approximately $1,500, providing students pick up the costs of their attire and footwear.

While it is not common practice, the ideas of giving high school credits for certain Fine Arts activities completed outside the walls of the school should be a serious consideration in most progressive schools. At one time, students who had passed the Grade 8 piano "conservatory exam," in Ontario were granted an extra high school credit, which was fully accepted by most universities in Canada. Many students can demonstrate Dance, Music, Drama, or Visual Arts at an expert level, and yet this learning is often overlooked.

Grappling with Ideas

- What are some fixed ideas about teaching ELA?
- Should the arts be integrated into other subjects and/or stand alone?
- What do you think might be worthy of additional credit in the arts?

Chapter 7

Science and Technology

It can be incredibly engaging when students experience the "hands-on" habits of a scientist's life. While learning to think, and interact like scientists with other scientists, is complicated, it is much more authentic than living inside a textbook. Unfortunately, there are far too many examples of dis-engagement that linger in the memory banks of students leaving Science and tech behind. Let's begin with the understanding that stuffing more Science facts into a student's brain is not the path to engagement. No question, students need to have access to key understandings, but let's not forget that technology can make such material readily available.

The "How to" books that line walls of bookstores list heaps of hands-on activities that can breathe life into a Science lesson. For instance, students can: design an amusement park; make an animal den; design a space colony; design and manage a greenhouse; hatch eggs; renovate an animal sanctuary or zoo; make ice cream; make furniture; design a future space station; design their own deck/cottage; create own insect project; make a toy factory; build a Rube Goldberg machine; create a model of the Canada Arm; build a robot; launch a rocket; conduct a Crime Scene Investigation (forensics); make a microwave oven; apply for a patent; make an instrument; make a bee box; make a watershed; build a monarch butterflies sanctuary; take part in a reducing roadkill project; create their own atom; build and fly a drone; make a brick; build a car or golf cart; design and build a tree fort; organize a Kickstarter campaign; or design an ideal hospital or school. Many of these ideas were gathered from books, blogs, Science association newsletters, and makerspace websites (makezine.com; facebook.com/MindShift.KQED/; kickstarter.com; 1001pallets.com), and often LinkedIn updates.

What tends to be missing from these lists is how to organize the ideas systematically, in such a way, that the experiences are not random, repetitive or missed. With so many possibilities, how can schools organize Science so that all students get a chance to experience most, if not all, of such engaging projects? The curriculum leader needs to do more than simply list options.

Professional Science Associations such as the National Science Teachers Association (NSTA) host annual conferences that feature innovative and engaging programming in Science education. A strong team of Science educators should have access to new ideas that reach beyond conventional textbooks.

An emphasis on STEM programming has brought serious attention to the solid ties between Technology, Engineering, Mathematics and Science. The "T" in STEM can be viewed as a separate discipline, but I would argue that technology is a tool; while it requires deliberate teaching, it needs to be applied in multiple discipline areas. While students need to learn how to use specific software such as Excel, PowerPoint, CAD, databases, and so on, the days of using technology only in a computer lab should be reconsidered.

The purchase of hardware can be an expensive proposition. Classrooms may be equipped with laptops, iPads, projectors, and printers, with limited or full access to the Internet. Projectors in each classroom are well worth the investment. Mounted projectors can cost between $500 and $1,000, but such costs are not repeated each year. In a small school with less than 200 students, classrooms can usually be equipped with projectors for approximately $15,000. Most schools have whiteboards, which when combined with projectors are far less expensive than "smartboard technology," which can cost upwards of $5,000 for each board (approximately $70,000 for a small school). Classrooms may have their own printers, but finding quality printing hardware that does not bleed the budget for replacing laser and ink cartridges is worthy of investigation. Ideally, schools can secure printers for about $1,000 per classroom. The use of 3D printers in schools can also enhance Science and arts programming. Average costs for such hardware can range between $500 and $,1000. It's important to check Consumer Reports to find out which products are more durable with fewer replacement and maintenance costs.

Schools can save money on maintenance costs by instituting a Bring Your Own Device (BYOD) policy. The idea stems from the notion that for students to be equipped in the twenty-first century, they need to be able to move their device between home and school. Schools would need to budget to provide financial support to bridge the gap for some students who cannot afford their own device. To save costs, Fullan and Langworthy (2014) noted that the *Magellan Initiative* in Portugal had parents contributing money toward technology based on a sliding scale of family incomes (p. 71). They added that "other means of collecting funds might be via property tax levies in the form of a Technology Levy."

Fullan and Langworthy (2014) noted that technology costs approximately $220 "less than 2% of the average $11,831 per student per year spent on education at the primary and secondary level in the US." Even when the United States has more than the OECD overall average spending per student ($8,595 per year), countries with considerably less are making technology "well within the range of feasibility" (p. 73). Countries such as Mexico, Portugal, and Turkey understand this, and are making some of the most ambitious efforts in the world to provide technology to all their students . . . there is literally no economic reason for it not to become a reality in the very near future (p. 73). They added: "what stands in the way of technological progress "is more a matter of political will than of economics" (p. 78).

It's important to have a curriculum plan in place so that the technological tools can serve to augment the academic program. The idea of *blended learning* combines classrooms with the web in a hybrid teaching methodology, which means that students are connecting with online courses while in school with their classmates. Originally, e-learning was developed to facilitate independent work, but more schools are blending such resources within the academic program.

We can do much more than offer laptops as digital notebooks. They can be tools for knowledge building. Innovative *Knowledge Forum* software emerged from the *Computer Supported Intentional Learning Environments* (CSILE) research in Canada. CSILE technology was designed as a medium for knowledge creation: "The heart of CSILE/Knowledge Forum is a multimedia community knowledge space. In the form of notes, participants contribute theories, working models, plans, evidence, reference material, and so forth to this shared space."[1]

Apart from online programming, schools can purchase a full assortment of software programs that support learning. With so many new apps available, it can be a full-time job to pilot and select which programs can support the curriculum. It takes a savvy technology coordinator to know how well certain software can link and enhance the academic program. Students can benefit from learning how to develop web pages and movies, as well as use different kinds of presentation software (i.e., *PowerPoint; Google Slides; SlideDog; Canva; Visme; Adobe Spark*, etc.). I have found that specific online programs, such as *Flocabulary, IXL, and Dreambox* (for Math), and *Middlebury Interactive* (World Languages) can augment subject-specific curriculum. MIT's *Scratch* coding experience is designed to "express creativity in new ways."[2] *Kaizena* is a new writing tool that "integrates with Google Classroom and allows for text feedback and recorded audio feedback."[3] *Perusall* is a collaborative reading program that directs students "to interact with the text at least five times in the form of questions . . . posed by peers, or by expanding on thinking."[4] While schools may budget for what they might be familiar with, it also makes sense to leave some wiggle room for funding and piloting new technology. Without draining the budget, schools can also use free web resources.

According to Fullan and Langworthy (2014), "new pedagogies could potentially deliver twice the learning for the same price or less" (p.68). They note that tablets can be roughly $200–$250: "The good news is that when purchased or leased in large quantities at the district, state or country level, device costs can be reduced further, and there is a high likelihood that prices will continue to decline" (p. 70). Their report recommends that schools need to provide students the technological tools they will need to thrive in the future. They note that the cost of technology "is coming down every day as price points for devices decrease, more high-quality learning resources become available online, and as teachers and students naturally become more digitally sophisticated in their everyday lives" (p. 68).

Keeping up with technology can be a full-time job. In fact, many schools have technology coordinators playing key roles on the curriculum team; such an investment in expertise is well worth the added expense. In cases where schools provide technology devices, it can be expensive to keep technology running smoothly. Fullan and Langworthy (2014) suggested that student tech teams have proven "to be an incredible source of strengthening and expanding device support, especially if students are well organized and trained by professional staff and have online support resources" (p. 71).

It's not enough for students to have access to software; student and teachers need to learn how to vet the value of websites. Teaching students how to think critically and examine the validity and reliability of information is not simply a matter of teaching a unit on technological literacy. According to Lynch (2017a): "Students should know how to spot unbiased, reliable information and . . . misleading content . . . instead of simply taking what is presented at face value." He warns: "Our students should know what the difference is between a Wikipedia page online and a peer-reviewed article on the same topic." Access to the Internet provides multiple opportunities to teach about critical thinking and varied perspective, and as such, it is an important resource to factor in when budgeting for tools for an ideal school.

As far as the "E" in STEM is concerned, the emphasis on Engineering is a popular way for teachers to inspire the teaching and learning of physical Science. Rather than gaze at 3D materials and properties in 2D textbooks, students can be engaged in 3D activity within "makerspace" and robotics challenges. Such "hands-on" Science need not be limited to the elementary school Science class, nor should such experiences be optional, available for a few who can participate in after school clubs.

Funding for Science classrooms includes the ongoing purchase of materials for biological and chemical experiments. For the most part, expenses for physical Science were more equipment maintenance. Microscopes often break down, and given the capacity of computers and digital cameras to enlarge images, schools are looking at replacing the needs for class sets of costly microscopes with more digital technology. Science materials might cost a school approximately $5,000 each year. Vibrant Science classes would also feature real books for the identification and classification of living things (i.e., *Field and Stream* guide books) and online reference manuals for construction projects that with a sampling of varied textbooks could amount to approximately $4,000.

Two of the most powerful Science learning programs that have resonated for me have been the *NASA Space Camp* experience and *First Robotics* competitions. Unfortunately, such programs tend not to be offered to all students. A fortunate few, who can afford to participate after school on a robotics team, or attend a week of space camp during a winter or spring break, tend to reap the benefits of such quality Science programming. Even though robotics equipment can be very expensive to stock for all students in a school, it is becoming more mainstream every day. The average price for a small school (less than 200 hundred students) could reach $40,000 if students worked in pairs on robots each year.

Incredible Science can happen without much cost. The *Future Scientists* Program in Texas emerged from a collaborative of fourth through twelfth-grade students, parents, and teachers "to participate directly in cutting-edge research on an insect called the corn earworm."[5] This pest causes more than $1 billion dollars' worth of damage to farms each year. He added, "Students make daily observations of the insect's life cycle. Then they design an experiment to help find new ways to control the insect's damage to crops. The students grow their own corn crop to study" (p. 62). The students also worked with the local USDA/ARS lab and its scientists.[6]

Kubota (2017) refers to the Fruchter's PBL Lab in her university Global Teamwork course, featuring hundreds of technologically driven schools and building designs. The course, which fosters "a growing and devoted community of students, industry mentors and alumni" integrates cutting-edge collaborative technologies while attracting top building design and construction talent who have "gone on to be change agents in education and industry." The students "use building-design programs . . . instantly share annotations on their design schematics and check how plans from each of their disciplines—architecture, structural and mechanical engineering, and construction management—are integrated."

High school students in Detroit, Michigan took part in research and tech project that was described by Drake (2012) as an exemplary practice in her book, *Creating Standards Based Integrated Curriculum.* Such an inquiry model costs little to implement but helped shape the students' capacity to conduct research by exploring possibilities, narrowing focus, gathering data, analyzing primary and secondary sources, generating findings, and educating others. Specifically students learned how to conduct primary source interviews, in addition to calculating and displaying quantitative data in an application of statistics and data management. Students were taught how to use *Survey Monkey,* while receiving deliberate instruction to become proficient at using Word, Excel, PowerPoint, IMovie, Basic CAD and Web design. The software costs can vary.

Supporting more engaging inquiry approaches in Science and other subject areas is worth changing the curriculum for, and finding funds, or re-directing funds to make such programs more commonplace.

Grappling with Ideas

- Given the vast amount of Science content and need for authentic "hands-on" laboratory experiences, why do you think time is limited for Science education in elementary schools?
- What do you think contributes to students dropping out of senior Science classes in high school?

NOTES

1. Scardamalia (2004, p. 2).
2. Schwartz (2017b).
3. Schwartz (2017c).
4. Schwartz (2017c)
5. Jemison (2016, p. 62)
6. Jemison (2016, p. 62).

Chapter 8

Pure Mathematics

Quality Mathematics curriculum should be informed by current research into the teaching and learning of Mathematics as well as professional Mathematics associations (i.e., the National Council of the Teachers of Mathematics (NCTM)). Math teacher leaders in schools, districts or state/provincial and national levels, use these understandings to make decisions about resources that can support best practices. Such resources may be found in print or digital form. Many textbooks are also informed by current research and professional affiliations, but it is important to clarify that a textbook is not a curriculum.

Schools that opt for *Saxon Math, Singapore Math, Everyday Math*, or *McGraw Hill Math*, for instance, often rotate to a new series every three to four years. Such a short shelf life can often be attributed in the United States to which publisher is awarded the contract for designing the standardized test for the coming year. This "changing of the textbook guards" can be a costly habit. Kits and consumables with multiple digital packages for each grade can range in costs from $100 to over $200 per student. Having sample texts from different publishers can help Math teachers coordinate a comprehensive curriculum. Teachers can also design learning logs with built-in checks for understanding, as well as digital links to games, quizzes, and fun activities, all for a low cost of about $30 per student. In a small school, costs for using customized learning logs could amount to $5000, much less than the cost of conventional commercial texts that would be approximately $14,000–$28,000.

While Math specialists agree that using manipulatives can be value added, the use of cubes, rods, and a full complement of hands-on materials, often lay idle in classrooms. The costs for updating and maintaining such materials should be minimal, possibly within a $500 limit for small schools. Students can also benefit by having access to Math online subscriptions. Specifically, some approximate costs for popular interactive digital programs that augment Math learning include Dreambox ($4,000) and IXL ($2,100).

A quality Math curriculum must account for current research. Games in the Math classrooms can add so much to an engaging learning environment. Burns (2017) noted that many teachers incorporate Math games into their daily instruction, and some encourage game play with families for homework. Many Mathematics programs have embedded chess and other card and board games into their courses, as engaging ways to apply mathematical understandings. Finding new board games each year to promote Math understandings is a worthwhile investment. Teachers can refresh a strong games activities center by budgeting for an estimate $500 a year for each Math classroom.

Rosholm, Bjørnskov, Mikkelsen, and Gumede (2017) examined what happened when a weekly lecture of traditional Mathematics was replaced with chess instruction. They concluded that chess "tended to increase subsequent results in math test scores." They discovered that chess instruction "reduced boredom and increased happiness" when unhappy students were given the opportunity to participate in chess as part of their Mathematics classes. The scores on the local standardized math test went up 10% after integrating chess into the curriculum. Vinyl chess sets can cost upwards of $18. In a school with 140 chess players, the budget for starting a chess program for all students in third through twelfth grade would start at around $1,100. Otherwise, maintaining a chess program would be a minimal replacement cost for lost materials.

A quality Mathematics curriculum embraces students speaking about and with others. Holly Pond Middle School adopted the popular *Shark Tank* program as a medium for using Math in the context of entrepreneurship projects. Moore (2015) noted that students acted as "aspiring entrepreneurs to pitch their business proposals to a panel of "shark" investors," and added: "Successful pitches require rock solid research and the ability to communicate an idea clearly and successfully." Apart from speaking Math and pitching ideas, a strong Math curriculum should include the teaching of financial literacy.

Teachers can also think about creative ways to celebrate special days, such as *Pi Day*. March 14 is the day Einstein was born and physicist Stephen Hawking passed away. The notion of Pi (Greek letter "π") that can be "calculated to over 1 trillion digits beyond the decimal point" can lead to different kinds of investigations. Apart from calculating the diameter or ratio of the circumference of a circle, this irrational number "will continue infinitely without repetition or pattern" (piday.org).

Recognizing that patterning in Math, is fundamental, the idea of teaching coding as a series of patterns has received much attention, not so much as a part of Mathematics, but as part of a separate technology course. Tepylo and Floyd (2018) wrote about the value of coding for Mathematics: "By using rich problems, where students require specific programming commands that are mathematical in nature; and by explicitly discussing the mathematics inherent to the programming commands, our students improve their understanding of the mathematics and programming concepts." The notion of teaching computer science within more complex Mathematics patterning units makes good sense. Burt (2014) shared his disappointment that there was little mention of Math on the Code.org website: he suggested that there are numerous ways for bringing coding into the Math classroom that have not been addressed in the *Common Core State Standards*:

- output and printing to screen teaches concepts like Cartesian plotting, graphing functions and conics;
- using the logic of loops . . . to teach principals of proofs;
- number sense—integers, floating/rounding, and how using the wrong data type affects programming; and,
- writing simple programs to solve the quadratic formula, the midpoint theorem, and . . . automating the rote memorization processes we've been drilling and killing for years.

What appears to stand in the way of "revision-ing" the possibility of coding as a part of Mathematics is perhaps the lag in helping all teachers understand how to code and how to teach it. Burt (2014) recognized that schools do not teach computer science courses because "there aren't enough qualified educators out there to meet the demands." He claimed that schools just need to provide a small amount of preparation to build a "trained army of math teachers out there willing to find new and better ways of delivering their content."

While coding experiences have been developed in a sense as "add-ons," we need to think how we can better synthesize more relevant and engaging experiences within the context of the Mathematics curriculum. The estimated costs for the Code.org program is $1 for each elementary student, $8 for middle-school-aged students and $33 for high school-aged students. In a school of 160, if all students were taking part in such an experience, the cost would be approximately $2000. Professional training or development for teachers can range between $4,400 for high school educators, and $2,300 for middle school Math teachers. Training for each elementary educator was listed at $150.

A quality Mathematics program for students in PK through twelfth grade is one that leads to mastery of key concepts and understandings. Many experts support the use of multiple learning tools for enhancing the learning of Mathematics. The costs associated with the development of learning logs, the use of manipulatives, engagement in online subscriptions, the integration of chess and coding can amount to approximately $15,000 each year.

Grappling with Ideas

- Teaching a data and statistics unit within a research-based course, separate from the conventional teaching of Mathematics, is a different approach. What would be the advantages and disadvantages of such a change?
- Teaching measurement within Science courses would be a new approach. What might be the barriers and benefits to reducing the number of units in a Mathematics curriculum?
- Teacher aspects of computer science within Mathematics courses would be a new approach. What might be the benefits and challenges for students and teachers?
- Who should teach Mathematics in elementary and high schools?

Chapter 9

Physical Education

Fitness activities, team sports, racquet sports, gymnastics, martial arts, rowing, track and field, and a host of other nonconventional sports, such as frisbee golf, are samples of organized contexts for learning about physical intelligence. There are many reasons a quality daily Physical Education program is part of a great school. Gardner (1985) spoke to the notion that Physical Education plays a role in one's overall intelligence:

> A description of the use of the body as a form of intelligence may at first jar . . . This divorce between the mental and physical has not infrequently been coupled with the notion that what we do with our bodies is somehow less privileged, less special, than those problem-solving routines carried out chiefly through the use of language, logic or some other relatively abstract symbolic system. (pp. 207–208)

Physical ways of knowing poses its own abstract and tactile way of making sense in the world. Even when it makes sense that we educate the whole child, there are forces in education that pay lip service to this critical part of a balanced education. According to PHE Canada, physically literate individuals "move with competence and confidence in a wide variety of physical activities in multiple environments that benefit the healthy development of the whole person."[1]

Often students take part in intensive athletic programming outside of school. Young gymnasts can be training upwards of twenty-four hours per week; swimmers can be in the pool twice a day. While some sports schools try to support these students, it is rare that such students are granted reduced course loads or assignments, which can add to the sleep deprivation problems that complicate the lives of many young athletes. While some jurisdictions may create special sports schools, it is uncommon for credits to be awarded for expert experience outside school. Even students who have taken rigorous lifeguard training or have achieved black belts in distinguished martial arts are rarely afforded Physical Education credits for their exemplary work in the field.

Dance is an area of Physical Education, and while it crosses over into the arts, it holds a significant place in the mastery of movement. Mastering the different forms of dance can be challenging for the typical Physical Education teacher. How often do we see a volleyball coach teaching ballroom, folk, ballet, modern, jazz or tap dancing? Unfortunately, many students do not have the opportunity to experience the full range of dance classes in school; rather, such expertise lies in community programs outside the walls of the school, for those who can afford such instruction.

Ideally, schools will provide a physical medium for students to acquire lifelong active habits. To develop an appreciation for active lifestyles, physical activity needs to be a daily activity, beyond a fifteen break at recess. A key way PHE Canada supports the necessity for Physical Education is by defining and promoting Quality Daily Physical Education (QDPE) as a: "well-planned school program of compulsory physical education provided for a minimum of 30 minutes each day to all students (kindergarten to grade 12) throughout the school year."

Most Physical Education curriculum can be grounded in either a movement approach to learning or a coaching focus on sport development. Many physical educators are former athletes, and as such, they tend to approach the subject matter from a coaching perspective. The movement approach to Physical Education tends to be more commonplace within a primary program. It has deeps roots in Laban's theory (1947) of human movement. Rudolf Laban's theory focuses on the body, space, effort, and relationship groupings.[2]

Fitness activities tend to be key components of warm-ups or warm/cool downs; a quality fitness program would address a balance of cardiovascular, muscular strength, endurance, and flexibility exercises. Students should also take part in fitness warm-ups, game, and activity design. Beginning with the plans, examining the implementation, realizing the limitations, and then revising the games/activities, helps students build a repertoire of creative physical ways of learning.

Physical Education programming can also incorporate outdoor education with specific skills and habits afforded to such activities as canoeing, backpacking, paddle boarding, kayaking, sailing, snowshoeing, skiing, biking, climbing, golf, rowing, and orienteering. A quality Physical Education program would support young people learning to acquire lifelong physical skills for leisure and health benefits.

Does it cost more to ensure students experience a comprehensive Physical Education program? Apart from hiring qualified teachers, the costs for a quality PE program rests with the replacement of equipment, that may require an estimated $2,000 each year for maintenance. The costs for Varsity teams and intramural programs would be much higher, but these investments would fall under a different "school life" or "extra-curricular" layer of a school budget.

Grappling with Ideas

- Discuss why Physical Education should be a course taken each year in high school.
- Do you think physical intelligence contributes to one's overall intelligence?

NOTES

1. phecanada.ca.
2. Smith (1994, p. 15).

Chapter 10

Classroom Assessment and Standardized Testing

Assessment is part of curriculum, and given we entrust teachers with the responsibility of implementing curriculum, it is important to pay particular attention to how teachers assess their students. Systems that expect teachers to follow a textbook or commercial program as the "curriculum" are less inclined to trust teachers to measure the growth of their students. In such cases, more value is placed on assessment tools developed outside the classroom context. It could be argued that teachers in such scenarios give up their professionalism when the thinking and designing of lessons and expert observations are removed from their job descriptions. In such cases, the standardized testing movement and the accompanying test practice curriculum has morphed teachers into technicians, not trusted or considered capable of developing curriculum. The cost of having the curriculum developed outside the classroom and separate from the teacher is at odds with a quality education. Rather than developing teachers as professionals, that is—curriculum designers and expert assessors, many systems reduce the role, to an almost automated process of manufactured learning. The costs of learning loss when teachers are relegated to technician roles have yet to be studied, but the lack of young people interested in becoming teachers and the number of young people leaving the profession is alarming.

Creating commercial resources with ready-made tests for classroom teachers is a lucrative business. One school in DC with just over 400 students spent close to $800,000 on textbooks and commercial materials. Even when such programs were in place, the school added over $25,000 for a practice test preparation program. Such costs could amount to the addition of 15 teachers working with students in a 12:1 student–teacher ratio—rather than the 20:1 student ratio.

Furthermore, the added costs of standardized tests, for the sake of ranking students and schools, needs to be revisited. Is it an assumption that our teachers are not capable of assessing the students in their own classroom? What purpose does it serve to rank them against other students who reside in different zip codes?

According to Darling-Hammond:

> States currently spend about . . . $25 per pupil . . . on assessments that have been found to be of relatively low quality, yet they base many decisions on these tests, thus focusing schools' efforts almost exclusively on low-level skills. Ironically, local districts spend even more on test preparation, plus interim and benchmark tests aimed at improving performance on the state tests, bringing total spending to over $50 per pupil. This spending does not improve higher-order learning . . . nearly all of it is geared toward boosting scores on multiple-choice tests.

Lynch (2018) questioned school cultures where students work inside individual test packets "filling in bubbles on scan sheets with sharpened pencils." He added: "the tests are virtually the same boring layout that they were when many of us took our standardized tests as K-12 students." Students can be exposed to standardized tests designed to gather comparative data at the classroom, school, district, state, national or international levels, but making such testing the central goal of education should not be the emphasis in schools.

Readiness for College and Careers (PARCC) testing was developed to see how to make improvements in the *Common Core State Standards*. When such initiatives are tied to funding, it can lead schools to worship a "practice testing" model of curriculum. According to Lynch (2016a), "Teachers find themselves stuck in a no-win situation . . . where they must reach certain benchmarks to receive recognition and funding." He added, "they have to forsake learning in wider scopes to make it happen." Given that testing and practice testing have engulfed and re-shaped the curriculum in a way that overrides greatness, the necessity of such practices must be challenged. As Lynch (2017b) claimed: "For many teachers, the way that they want to teach and the way that they are forced to teach vary greatly, and much of that is due to unreasonable accountability standards that include student performance on standardized tests."

The EQAO tests in Ontario were developed as accountability measures. In 2014, the cost of the test to administer was $30 million; six years later the focus on testing and accountability has increased to over $100,000. Experts have advised the government to eliminate this testing, test on two or three year cycles or move to random sampling of testing. Removing annual testing would also slow down the grind of having practice tests bleed so far into the fabric of teaching. There is little time to learn when students are being tested so much. In addition to budgeting for EQAO testing, there are over 80 student achievement officers assigned to school boards that duplicate the costs of existing consultants to the tune of over $14 million each year.

The SAT and the ACT (American College Testing) are probably the most familiar standardized tests that are typically used to gain university entrance. Both tests cover a broad range of questions, but one notable difference is that the ACT does not subtract wrong from right answers. While both test results function to help school admission teams send out their offers of acceptance, they are not a comprehensive measure of student achievement. Most college admission departments indicate that standardized test scores are only one metric they consider.

The collateral damage of high stakes testing affects students in different ways. The pressure to achieve can be so overwhelming for young people. Kamenetz (2017) was concerned about close to three million stressed-out high school students taking the AP exams. She noted that such courses are perceived as "a mark of the aspirational, a promise of higher standards and, occasionally, a more expensive alternative." The claim that such coursework offers a higher-end education has yet to be proven: "remarkably little independent research has been conducted on the academic benefits of AP."[1] Regardless of undocumented evidence of benefits, there is little doubt the business of testing is a lucrative one. Referring to the recent boom in AP popularity, Kamenetz (2017) noted that "it costs $93 to take the "AP" exam, plus often hundreds of dollars for textbooks and lab fees."

On a global scale, the Program of International Student Assessment (PISA) conducts tests every three years. Upwards of half a million students take this two-hour survey that evaluates education systems worldwide. In 2012, PISA results ranked the United States below Finland, various European nations, Asian countries, Canada, and Australia.[2] By 2015, the United States ranked 31st among the 35 Organization for Economic Cooperation Development (OECD) industrialized member nations,[3] putting the United States in the bottom 11.4% of these nations. The cost of the PISA assessment is approximately $25 million to administer in the United States. Comparatively, the National Assessment of Educational Progress (NAEP) in 2011, costs $129 million. Across 25 U.S. states, combined spending is tallied at $669 million per year, with a total cost of over 1.7 billion/year for all 50 states.[4] It seems to be in the best of interest of some people to support the standardized testing movement.

An education system with a rudder firmly focused on high stakes testing, misses the mark on deep learning and preparing young people to be innovators in the future. As Fullan and Langworthy (2014) so elegantly claimed: "whole system change still faces significant barriers in most places. These barriers reside primarily in the student assessment, teacher evaluation and school accountability regimes that currently define success for our education systems." They further suggested: "Until we find new ways to define and measure success—ways that measure schools' adoption of new pedagogies and students' achievement of deep learning outcomes—crucial system factors will stand in opposition to innovation" (p. 3).

There are many strong voices who challenge the over-reliance of testing. Lynch (2016b) claimed: "Assessments turn living, breathing students into machines, of sorts, who must be programmed to spit out the right answers at the right time." Sornson (2017a) pointed out that many systems have failed to improve scores, yet what remains is the push toward "more standardized, superficial, fragmented and meaningless learning" (p. 4). In another article, he noted, "We deliver more content than is reasonable in the time allowed, hoping that by "covering" the standards that might be included on the mandated assessments our students will get better test scores" (2017b, p. 2).

And how can anyone be so sure that these results actual measure what students know? People should not view the results of standardized slices as full specimens of learning, when such results represent a small cell of a much larger learning organism. Schwartz (2014) concluded that such tests "don't measure effective oral communication, collaboration, learning how to learn or develop academic mindsets." And Lynch (2017c) claimed: "Not all students are natural-born test takers," so to assume that standardized tests have captured the learning is simply naïve.

Standardized tests should also be subject to accountability measures. Lynch (2016a) noted: "How can all students be measured with the same yardstick—and how can punishments and rewards be handed out using such a scale?" with a significant conclusion: "standardized assessments are flawed." He revealed the following issues embedded in the blind acceptance of standardized testing:

- Inadequate sampling of material being tested;
- Indirect, rather than direct, observation of what a student is truly learning;
- Too narrow a scope of knowledge;
- Not enough exceptions made for regional/cultural differences within a state;
- Too many lasting inferences made about the students taking the tests that are based on very little merit;
- Too much emphasis on a punishment mentality, and not enough on what can actually be improved; and,
- No accounting for socioeconomic or disadvantaged barriers that hinder a teacher's potential.

Relying on a single cell of an organism to shed light on the entirety of school learning, and using that data to define and compare greatness, is frankly sloppy analysis. In the long run, it can only serve to diminish a society's intellectual return. An investment of time to garner a true picture of learning needs to be the priority. Recognizing the need for balanced assessment, Stiggins (2008) noted: "We have come to a tipping point in American education when we must change our assessment beliefs" (p. 1). Concerned that decades of obsessive reliance on standardized tests has not been enough, he added, "The time has come to acknowledge the extreme limitations of these tests" (p. 2).

Finally, why are universities buying into such narrow indicators when admitting students? Rejecting more students does not equate to academic rigor. Low percentages of acceptances should not correlate as some status symbol. How we assess students reflects our teaching values. Quality classroom assessment is complex, and therefore takes time to unpack.

Grappling with Ideas

- How often should we assess?
- How much should we invest in testing? Can we save on assessment costs?
- How can leadership at the post-secondary level become more aware and think more deeply about assessment?
- Review this chapter and make a list of assessment practices you currently do, and a list of ideas for improving those practices.

NOTES

1. Warne (2017).
2. Lurie (2013).
3. Barshay (2016).
4. http://international-assessments.org/is-pisa-worth-its-cost-some-challenges-facing-cost-benefit-analysis-of-ilsas/

Chapter 11

Reducing Class Size

No doubt all classrooms aim to meet viable goals, but it helps when class sizes are small enough for quality individual support. Class size matters, not as a convenience for teachers, but as a significant condition for improved learning. Based on a longitudinal study of over 10,000 children, Blatchford, Moriarty, Edmonds, and Martin (2002) found: "In small classes, more one-to-one teaching occurred, and more teaching took place overall. In general, the *University of London Class Size Study* indicates that more teacher support for learning was evident in smaller classes" (p. 3).

Schanzenbach (2014) claimed that the "critics" of small classes were mistaken. "Class size matters. Class size is one of the most-studied education policies, and an extremely rigorous body of research demonstrates the importance of class size in positively influencing student achievement" (p. 4). She also claimed that increasing class size comes at a cost:

> all else being equal, increasing class sizes will harm student outcomes . . . Money saved today by increasing class sizes will result in more substantial social and educational costs in the future . . . While lower class size has a demonstrable cost, it may prove the more cost-effective policy overall. (p. 3)

The more students in a class, the more the impact of the teacher is diminished. According to Schanzenbach (2014), smaller classes are linked to higher achievement and this comes from a mix of: "higher levels of student engagement, increased time on task, and the opportunity small classes provide for high-quality teachers to better tailor their instruction to the students in the class." She added: "The research is there. Class size matters. Even the finest teachers are limited in what they can do when they have large classes. So can we stop pretending that class size doesn't matter."

Ted Sizer, former Harvard Dean of Education (1988) stated that high school teachers should not be responsible for more than 80 students: "bringing those ratios down . . . means drastically simplifying a school's program" (p. 31). It makes sense to question the quality of the research that supports large classes. Such research runs counter to the most current understandings in teaching and learning. Lave and Wenger (2002) coined the term "Legitimate Peripheral Participation" (LPP), as a process "by which newcomers become part of a community of practice . . . the mastery of knowledge and skills requires newcomers to move toward full participation in a community" (p.29). Smaller classes can enable more learners to shift through legitimate participation from novice to expert levels of knowing.

The constructivist approach that supports students building knowledge is enhanced when the learner talks with, and like, an expert. The teacher, in fitting with Vygotsky's notion of the "zone of proximal development" (ZPD), needs to be in direct proximity to the students, with ample time to help students transform their understandings from novice to more expert levels. Ideal classrooms can address the varied needs through differentiated instruction within the ZPD. When novices can speak and work with subject matter experts, they can apprentice into the world of expertise and be better prepared as future mathematicians, journalists, architects, artists, athletes, and so on.

Classic research, dating back to the early seventies,[1] points to the observation that teachers talk too much in the classroom setting. Even though we have been acutely aware of this research for nearly half a century, many teachers tend to talk for about two-thirds of the classroom time. As Fisher, Frey, and Rothenberg (2008) noted: "*Telling* students what you want them to know is certainly a faster way of addressing standards. But *telling* does not necessarily equate to *learning*" (p. 4). Smaller classrooms enable students to elaborate about texts and thus, talk more, represent better ideal learning conditions than teacher-directed environments. Keeping class sizes under 16 creates ideal conditions for students to speak for at least 70% of the time.

Many school missions claim that the school meets the needs of all students, but the more we squeeze too many students into classrooms, the more we minimize the possibility of ensuring high education returns. The costs of reducing class sizes can be significant, but the opportunity for enhanced learning is well worth the investment for both students and teachers.

It is possible to teach more students when the teacher does not individualize the curriculum by assuming that a "one size fits all" approach is good enough. Fullan and Langworthy (2014) noted, however, that "the biggest waste of all is the hours, days, years and decades squandered on boredom and alienation. If time is money, we have the opportunity to become billionaires in learning" (p. 74). There are too many expectations listed for learning at each grade level. The idea of covering expectations runs counter to ideal learning conditions.

When students take responsibility for teaching a classmate, they must ensure they have a solid understanding themselves. Peer teaching is a powerful learning experience that enables students to learn by teaching. In such roles, the peer teachers also consolidate their own understandings. As Barnes (1976) so elegantly noted: "Many a teacher has said that he did not fully understand some parts of his subject until he came to teach it" (p. 10). According to Scardamelia and Bereiter (1994), students who typically have difficulties describing a mental task "often come forth with clear statements of procedure when asked to give advice to another student, particularly a younger one, for carrying out the task" (p. 16).

While many educators agree that teaching is the best way to learn, few schools organize classes and schedules to accommodate for regular peer teaching programming. The cost of using cooperative, reciprocal, or peer teaching learning approaches is time, time for students to speak with one another and time for staff to learn more about such progressive practices. Carving time out of a busy schedule for students to learn about how to teach others is not easy, but the benefits—priceless.

Grappling with Ideas

- How do you think schools can reduce teacher: student ratios?
- What are ways you can encourage teachers to revise curriculum to enable more interactions in the zone of proximal development?
- How can Professional Development time be used to support the need for small classes?

NOTE

1. Flanders (1970).

Chapter 12

Scheduling for Change

The state of school schedules is at the core of school readiness to embrace change. As Watts and Castle (1993) noted: "You can implement any innovation you want in your classroom as long as you don't mess with the schedule. Traditional inflexible scheduling is based on administrative and institutional needs" (p. 306). It is much easier for schools to introduce innovative programs when schedule makers have permission to change existing structures. Often it is easier for schools to operate with predictable timetables, but the degree to which schedules are fixed, can determine whether, or not, a school is ready for change. How the program is carved up for students and teachers and the use of the physical plant, reflects both values and the key human capital costs at the school level. Much like a budget reveals a school's values, a schedule can, too. Goodlad (1984) claimed that "time is virtually the most important resource" in education (p. 30).

SCHOOL CALENDAR

The school calendar can be strategically timed for meaningful learning. Academic leaders in schools play a key role in determining the school calendar. The timing of breaks for individual schools in the public system is usually determined at the district or board level, whereas, charter, private or independent schools tend to have more flexibility. Student learning, at the mercy of statutory and religious holidays, is often disrupted. It can take its toll on a smooth academic experience.

Many students in elementary and high school struggle to juggle seven or eight subjects at one time, losing the opportunity to concentrate and apply learning. School policy makers, according to Levine (2002), should be more aware that long-term memory "works best when there's sufficient time for consolidation." He added:

> This does not occur when you partake of social studies for forty minutes followed by algebra for forty minutes, then English for forty minutes, and immediately thereafter physical education. Switching from one subject to another pretty much prevents the consolidation of the one that preceded it. (p. 118)

While having lengthier ninety-minute classes every other day in a "block schedule" is better than seven or eight subjects in a day, students still must manage the study of too many subjects at the same time during the school year. It is more authentic for students to focus on fewer areas to master. We do not ask adults to develop in seven or more distinct areas at the same time, nor do we ask teachers to teach seven or eight different subjects. Why should we expect students to manage such an academic load? It seems that the current system drowns students in too many diverse disciplines at the same time, which must limit their capacity to generate a high GPA.

Recognizing the need for students to focus on fewer subjects at a time, the Lawrence Park Blyth School in Toronto offers a four-term, two-course approach which "mimics the academic structure of post-secondary education." Table 12.1 outlines this concentrated duo-subject schedule:

Students in Grades 11 and 12 are scheduled for two credits at a time with the third period open for independent study (Grades 11 and 12) and a Foundations class (Grades 9 and 10). Such a schedule is one that supports student learning. "Our students," according to the Blyth website, "are able to manage their academic workload much more effectively."[1]

Schools eager to increase the critical mass of "knowing" students ready for college and life should reconsider the idea of semester programming. It's time to challenge "block scheduling" and recognize that it perpetuates a superficial smattering of teaching and learning, and the need for students to find alternative sources, either through technology or tutoring support, to gain a solid understanding of all the expectations in so many subjects at one time. Decisions about scheduling should be more about what serves students better.

Table 12.1 Blyth School Concentrated Duo-Subject Schedule

Period	Time
Period 1	8:40 a.m.–10:55 a.m.
Period 2	11:00 a.m.–1:10 p.m.
Lunch	1:15 p.m.–1:45 p.m.
Period 3	1:45 p.m.–4:00 p.m.

A schedule is sometimes a key variable overlooked when it comes to implementing change. Often reformers will have ideas cut short if their innovation cannot fit within the current schedule. Such an organizing force can be viewed as a fixed piece of school, often protected as some sacred framework, in other words, an obstacle to change. Rather than adopting existing schedules that are laden with prevailing values, it's important to learn how a framework can be built, beginning with the learners in mind. A flexible schedule can make room for multiage learning, internships opportunities and an expanded range of elective and co-curricular offerings. The cost of such change, an open mindset.

MULTI-AGE LEARNING

We live in a multi-age world, yet we place students in artificial grade groupings. Multi-grade and age classrooms can be highly effective learning environments. Students can work at their own pace. Teachers can stay with students (looping) for several years, so teachers have more time to minimize learning that otherwise might be left behind. Students who may not master multiplication, for instance, in grade 3, would have the same teacher in grade 4, able to keep what might not have been mastered on a bucket list—leaving fewer gaps behind. Different teachers also have different cultures and routines, and in conventional schools, students must adapt each year to a new teacher; in a multigrade classroom, time is not wasted at the start of the year, learning a "new teacher." The teacher simply picks up where the student left off.

The research on multi-age and multi-grade classrooms reveals that students show increased self-esteem, more cooperative behavior, better attitudes toward school in general, increased pro-social (caring, tolerant, patient, supportive) behavior, enriched personal relationships, increased personal responsibility, and a decline in discipline problems (Mackey, Johnson & Wood; Stone; Anderson & Pavin; Uphoff & Evans; Grant; Gutierrez & Slavin; Lodish; Katz, Evangelou & Hartman; Miller; Villa & Thousand; Pratt).

Many small schools begin with multi-age grades, or some schools use a split-grade model, in response to economic pressures, and while it can save education costs, the value of multi-age learning can be lost when teachers try to teach two different grades at the same time. A multi-grade approach to schooling has built-in differentiation so that students can work at their own level while engaging in the same project at the same time. In a split classroom, the teacher might be expected to have students work on two completely different themes, making the learning community divided by some artificial wall.

The lack of resources for multi-grade classrooms and sample schedules can be a challenge at first. In multi-age classrooms, teachers do not rely on textbooks as recipes; rather, these professional educators generate and design customized curriculum to serve the varied needs of their students. It is far less expensive to organize staffing for multi-age classrooms. Given the widespread benefits of multi-grade learning, it is surprising that there are only a few schools that embrace such practice. Designing such classrooms can impact the whole school. The benefits for students, of moving to such a progressive design, however, are well worth the time invested in professional conversations and parent education.

MAKING ROOM FOR INTERNSHIPS

Future School Superintendent, Trish Flanagan, spoke with pride about the value of internships. She spoke about fifteen-year-old Mario's experience with his CFO mentor of a local multimillion-dollar oil and gas company. She noted: "Often, we underestimate young people . . . we don't trust someone who is five, ten, or fifteen years old to be committed, determined, and have good ideas."[2] Many great learning opportunities can reside beyond the boundaries of school, yet when they penetrate the traditional school schedule, such ideas can be perceived as treading on sacred territory. The costs of change can be complicated, but schools can budget for transportation to and from internships, with long-term benefits far reaching.

INTERSESSION AND CO-CURRICULAR OPTIONS

Intersession programming can bring fresh experiences to the table in the form of options or electives. Students might engage in an immersed second language learning opportunity, take workshops or courses in Yearbook Design, Stock Market Trading, Film Production, Architecture or Home Construction. Students can use intersession time to extend research projects, sign up for additional AP courses or tinker in maker spaces to build inventions such as solar cars, new running shoes, or a new wave kitchen appliance with 3D printers. The costs of building in intersession programming may not be as expensive as one might assume. It might also be a way for generating revenue if community members pay to participate in special programs, as well.

At the school level, certain programs may define a specific niche of the school as well as the need for a distinct schedule. The struggle for change can be a challenge when it comes to bringing about consensus and the capacity of a staff for implementing new directions. It is often easier to open a new school with a clearly defined program such as Montessori Education or Enriched Montessori Schools; Reggio Emilia Education; International

Baccalaureate; Waldorf Education; Single Gender Schools (IBSC; NCGS); Forest Schools; Knowledge Building Schools (i.e., Institute of Child Study Laboratory School, Toronto, Canada); STEM Schools (engineering; environmental education; one hour of code); STEAM Schools (A for arts); Creativity Schools (i.e., Blue School, DaVinci Schools); and Character Education/Service Learning Schools (i.e., The Kindness School). Each of these schools grew out of a desire to change traditional schooling. Some schools may purchase such programs, and in some cases, identifying as a specific kind of school can require participation in a systematic accreditation process. Other schools may adopt aspects of a certain program, and thus proclaim to be more "inspired" or informed by the ideas. It's important to pay attention to how the schedule can be an important variable for school change.

Grappling with Ideas

- How often do staff sit down for schedule talks and address timetable options?
- What advantages and disadvantages are in a Monday to Friday schedule?
- Who benefits from the organization of time at your school?
- When is it ideal to designate times for reporting student progress and parent conferencing?
- When are the best times for assemblies or field trips?
- When should staff have professional development days?
- When is the most ideal time to plan breaks?
- How can schools adjust so that students can learn outside our classroom walls?
- Is there an advantage to organizing year-round schools?

NOTES

1. https://blytheducation.com/blyth-academy/lawrence-park/
2. Flanagan (2017).

Chapter 13

Staffing and Meaningful Roles

In many public school districts, the central office staff coordinate payroll, benefits, facility and safety maintenance, transportation, academic programming, information technology, legal work, and public relations/marketing. An efficient central office should ultimately reduce the administrative load at the individual school level. District office staff often determine formulas for staffing schools with teachers based on examining demographic data within each school boundary. School occupancy rates, as well as the teacher–student ratios, are often set from ranges established by district and state/provincial requirements. Many systems, including the distribution of funding happen at the Central office or higher-level order. The core value of equity guides such school decisions, at the same time as limits the range of possibilities for staffing for innovative schools.

It is not clear if there are savings with fewer central offices, and if so, if such savings outweigh the educational return associated with replicating the "sameness" in school operations and the budgets that support them. A clear view of the actual funds saved through expansion would be an important read for decision makers in education. The generation of "kingdoms" or departments, with assistants, and administrative staff within these district offices, should also be the focus of ongoing fiscal scrutiny. Rather than one person responsible for transportation in a school or smaller board, larger boards requires a transportation department. How do we know that there were cost savings at the district level without a clear view of the comparative data?

STAFFING IN SCHOOLS

The design of collective agreements in the public system or contracts for teachers in the independent, charter or private schools can set precedence in terms of defining staffing roles and responsibilities. Schools are ripe for embracing innovation when they can strategically revise all variables for change, including staffing.

Typically, elementary schools hire strong English Language Arts (ELA) teachers, but it can be challenging to match the work force with passionate Science, Technology, Engineering and Math educators; qualified STEM teachers tend to be more present in a high school setting. The traditional model with the homeroom teacher responsible for six or more disciplines, may seem comfortable for younger students (to not be on a "rotary" system with multiple teachers), but the overreliance on such an approach seems flawed.

Teachers, who can plan and implement fewer subjects, have more opportunities to generate student expertise as well as provide more effective remediation or enrichment. Examples of innovative schools exist where Kindergarten students spend half of the day with an expert Science-Math teacher and the other half of the day with a liberal arts teacher. Strong STEM or liberal arts teachers have an opportunity in these situations to influence more students, rather than a single class. Rather than see the choices as one teacher verses six teachers, it can be advantageous for schools to consider using pairings of teachers that can share multiple talents at the same time. Having a mix of "teaching" administrators, can also enable the school to reduce teacher: student ratios in each class.

RESIDENCIES AND INDUCTION

Staffing can be augmented by inviting student teachers, who share current research and best practices into the school community. Colleges of Education can team with local schools to support preservice learning, as well as induction programming. Different kinds of relationships can be established to support new teachers to further develop their capacities in the contexts of classrooms. Some schools provide "residencies" in much the same way as young physicians are introduced to the medical profession. DeMoss (2016) noted that there have been dramatic improvements in countries such as Finland and Singapore: "one of the shifts their nations embraced was to integrate teacher preparation with K-12 school systems. Aspiring teachers are paid to practice under the guidance of an effective classroom teacher for a full year" (p. 6).

Concerned about new teachers in the field, Dean Moje at the University of Michigan claimed that it is difficult to support young teachers who they are moved from classroom to classroom: "they can't get their feet under them."[1] The limited notion of "ready-made" teachers leaving teacher's college is now a misconception. The development of a teacher does not end on the final day of college teacher preparation; rather, this stage of development is a beginning, and when systems organize schools as learner organizations for staff and students, the quality of teachers should continue to improve. Schools that build relationships with colleges of education, can help extend induction type programs, so that teachers stay in the profession, rather than be thrown into the deep end without a life jacket to support them.

Furthermore, the need for quality induction programming needs to be a priority as the talent pool of young people interested in the profession is declining. At Michigan State University, enrollment for teacher preparation programs was down by approximately 35%, "and as much as 45% at the University of Michigan." According to each program head, "the decline is so steep, the impact on the teacher prep pipeline so great, that there is an unavoidable personnel deficit lurking out there, exacerbated by the number of baby boomer-aged teachers approaching retirement." Costs need to be factored into budgets for added supports from colleges. In addition to providing field experiences for teachers in preparation programs, teaching and learning experts from different colleges of education can work directly with administrators, teachers, and students to pilot innovative programs. Schools need to expand their professional development budgets to cover the costs for such on-sight expert visits and more colleges of education will need to increase the number of staff and expand job descriptions to include room for induction responsibilities. Depending on specific induction needs of the school and research needs of college professors, schools could provide $15,000 or more in funding to have regular access to such curriculum and school operations expertise. Research conducted by Donaldson and Moore Johnson (2011) and later, Goldring, Taie, and Minsun (2014) claimed that: "20–70% of newly certified American teachers quit within five years chiefly because of heavy workload and low salary." Schools need to figure out how to keep talent in the teaching field. Schools need support to develop teachers beyond their initial teacher preparation experience.

RIGOROUS STAFF SELECTION PROCESS

A rigorous process for selecting teaching staff is central to nurturing a quality professional culture. Ideally the process should involve a thorough analysis of a resume and covering letter, a series of interviews, observation of sample teaching, reference follow through, and solid background checks. A comprehensive bank of interview questions can allow candidates time to explain how they can demonstrate their capacity to plan and create engaging curriculum, as well as instruct in multiple ways to meet the needs of different learners. Questions should also focus on how well candidates have developed relationships, and modeled being life-long learners.

To differentiate candidates, interviewers should not rush the process; being prepared to invest at least an hour of time to interview qualified candidates makes good sense. Ideally schools will have the autonomy to recruit incredible teachers with multiple talents. It is important for schools to develop a critical mass of teachers with a desire to learn and improve, exhibit growth mindsets and be ready and willing, to be supported, as well as being supportive of others. It can certainly be advantageous for a teacher to have a track record of moving students to positive action; and teacher–leaders, who are open to moving colleagues to action. Teacher candidates can be assets to solid school teams if they belong to professional organizations, engage in action research, and have a clear record of volunteerism.

The upfront work to find talent with a good fit for the school's mandate can minimize costs down the road. Doing some serious legwork can contribute to making good hiring decisions. Some schools may outsource the recruitment process, but ideally, school leaders should invest their time to manage this process, as well as save costs. In many schools, however, the principal is handed the staff roster from afar, with little or no say in the matter.

Grappling with Ideas

- What do you think are the most important aspects of a quality staffing process?
- What details shared in this chapter do you think are worthy of further review?
- How is it possible to increase the talent pool in schools?

NOTE

1. Kaffer (2017).

Chapter 14

Staff Development

A detailed look at the possibilities of staff development can provide rich options for change and innovation in schools. Without effective systems and budget support for staff development, a school will lack the foundation necessary to support change and innovation. Staff development is about supporting all teaching and noninstructional staff in a school.

Making a habit of gathering annual satisfaction surveys from students, families, and staff can aid in determining the focus of school wide staff development. There is also data of the quantitative and qualitative kind that can emerge from an examination of student work, staff accomplishments, and results from standardized and classroom testing. Such data should directly inform a school's long-term strategic plan and short-term school improvement plan, as well as staffing needs.

MENTOR MEETINGS AND CO-TEACHING

Building in regular times for new teachers to meet with each other, and at least one mentor, on a regular basis can be a very helpful addition to a strong staff development program. Often new teachers feel alone; they can single themselves out as the only ones not meeting their students' needs. Such meetings can boost confidence and provide a special space for novice teachers to have time to talk about their experiences. It is not always easy for new teachers to participate on even ground with seasoned teachers at staff meetings or other professional development activities. As a school leader, the weekly lunches with my novice teams also provided valuable input for how to better provide ongoing support.

In one school, we developed a more formal mentorship support system. We added to each teacher's schedule, an hour for team planning. During this time, the teacher mentors met in a 1:1 setting to plan a class that they would co-teach for an hour together, ideally the next day. Each week students would also benefit from having two teachers, one more seasoned, working with them in their classroom. Often the mentor teachers would teach model lessons, so the less experienced teachers could observe how new approaches could increase student engagement.

We began with approximately 20% of the staff demonstrating exceptional levels of performance. With this mentorship program in place, the critical mass of exceptional teachers shifted to 45% over the course of one year. Bringing together teachers in a regular classroom-based mentorship program also contributed to an increase in overall Math scores that rose 9% on average, in one academic school year.

Sharratt and Harild (2015) found that good leaders "build collaborative-lateral learning structures where teachers co-learn, co-teach, mentor, coach, and engage in meaningful professional conversations that are personalized to the improvement of their personalized practice" (p. 59). Team meetings coordinated within the school day can provide significant opportunities to talk and act about what each teacher can do to support each other. Many schools have budgets that support one or more full-time coaches, so the added expense for part-time teacher-leaders, who teach and mentor, would not be more than the added expense of coaching staff who are out of the classroom in many conventional schools today.

IN-HOUSE AND OFF-SITE PROFESSIONAL DEVELOPMENT

Schools need to provide opportunities for in-house and off-site professional development. Travel costs for off-site workshops can be expensive, so making room for school-based activities and online webinars or course work can be very effective options as well. At one school, we funded twelve staff members to attend *Harvard Project Zero*. $35,000 from the PD budget was directed to cover the cost of flights, accommodation, and registration. Upon return, these teachers coordinated a panel during our summer PD. It was incredible to witness the transformations. One teacher was asked to share her "take away" from *Project Zero*:

> This experience was an emotional one that allowed us to build on previous experiences and expand on our capabilities as educators. We were excited to share what we learned during our weeklong professional development before

the school year began, and arranged for small teacher study groups to learn about and implement the various skills we took from PZ. (Ms. L)

The goal of having a school 'crawling with teacher-leaders' was taking shape.

Frequently, funding for staff to attend conferences tends to be one of the first areas of the budget to be cut when times are tight. Ideally, staff members would be supported to the tune of $1,000 each for professional conference participation, especially if they were responsible for bringing home and sharing the ideas with the rest of the staff. We rewarded staff members with funds for international travel if they were selected to present at conferences; the bar was set high in that our teacher-leaders were expected to be more than conference delegates.

TAKING ON TEACHER LEADERSHIP ROLES

While most traditional leadership roles in schools tend to be distant from the classroom, they do not have to be. A school can support different leadership roles, and if these teacher-leaders are willing to take on a partial teaching schedule, there is more room to increase the number of lead positions. A teacher-leader might teach for half a day, leaving the other half of the day to team teach with teachers, as well as do specific job-embedded administrative work. Rather than the traditional model, where the principal and the assistant principal run around doing all things administrative, there are many more creative and affordable ways to assemble a team of teacher-leaders. As Ghandi suggested: "A good sign of a leader is not how many followers you have, but how many leaders you create."

Teachers can feel empowered in leadership roles. At one elementary arts school, rather than have two full-time "academic coaches," we created six new teacher-leader roles that supported 63 staff members and 440 students. The VP, School Culture was responsible for building a positive student and parent community climate, at the same time as providing oversight of disciplinary action and extracurricular programs, including special days and assemblies. The VP, Academics was responsible for vertical subject matter planning, as well as the coordination of resource orders; the VP, School Management was the point person for safety and facilities; the Dean of Special Education was responsible for ensuring all special needs supports were in compliance with local legislation; the Dean of Staff Development worked closely with the VP, Academics to provide ongoing professional development; and the Dean of Fine Arts supported all the in-house and guest arts teachers in Music, Visual Arts, Theater Arts, and Dance.

Most of these teacher-leaders taught their own students for at least half a day. By developing job-embedded leadership roles, rather than "assistants," teacher-leaders could focus on doing fewer responsibilities well. The cost of re-structuring to increase more teacher-leader roles can be augmented when staff can continue to be in classrooms on a part-time basis. With key teacher-leaders having a part-time teaching role, this would reduce the overall costs of teaching staff, as well.

A small school with three part-time teacher-administrators might require an additional $60,000 to support such hybrid responsible roles. Given that a single full-time assistant principal might require a six-figure salary, such an investment builds in additional leadership with at least three half teaching positions. Looking at salary expenses in this light could mean overall cost savings.

Having more teacher-leaders on board can also increase the hands available for providing performance reviews. School administrators can carve out at least one hour per day to teach, so they can understand and know their students as learners, and understand what teachers go through on a daily basis. A teaching principal can also contribute to reducing the t:s ratio, reducing the overall staffing costs and increasing more planning time for teachers. School leaders can model by example, the same great practice they expect from their teachers.

ENGAGING IN ACTION RESEARCH

With so many avenues for professional development, action research, is often put on the back burner, as an option for a select few teachers. In an ideal school, all teachers take part in gathering and analyzing data, and comparing it with existing educational research. Teachers can learn to systematically track the impact of transforming their teaching; in doing so, they have much to offer their students and education as a whole.

The depth and breadth of Jack Whitehead's (2018) work has encouraged "professional educators to consider the process of practitioner action research as a means to self-assessment, renewal and professional development" (p. 53). He argued that a teacher's systematic reflection of experience provides insights about their descriptions, and that we can accept such as explanations as valid accounts of their educational development (p. 9). Teachers, who become action researchers, according to Croft, Cogshall, Dolan, Powers, and Killion (2010):

> select an aspect of their teaching to systematically investigate, such as wait time during questioning. They record data and consider theories from the research

literature, draw conclusions about how teaching is influencing learning and vice versa, and inform future instructional decisions. (p. 6)

BECOMING CURRICULUM WRITERS AND REVIEWERS

Apart from offering mentoring, on-site workshops and conferencing experiences, staff members can be empowered by curriculum writer and reviewer roles. In one school, we deliberately set out to develop our own teaching resources:

> Rather than continue to repeat the cycle of purchasing materials, written by people not familiar with the school context, we chose to develop materials that would guide the teacher and the student at the same time. By empowering teachers with the skills and capacity to write curriculum for their students, we saved hundreds of thousands of dollars, and redirected the funds to decreasing the teacher-student ratio, giving students more individual attention.[1]

In this situation much more than improving test scores mattered: "Our plan was to build curriculum that would stick with the students." By making authentic materials, teachers increased their ownership over the curriculum and their commitment to implementing it.

Quality staff development requires qualitative analysis, and notably hard work. Technology may appear to make the process of continuous improvement easy, but there is no question, elbow grease is required. Investing in successful staff development involves time. School leaders with a hub of teacher-leaders can help ensure that all direct-reports have regular feedback and support to offer their best to the school. The cost of developing and sustaining quality staff development can require a re-purposing of funds. Without adequate support for change, most plans for innovation and school improvement will simply be words, without actions.

Grappling with Ideas

- Describe an effective professional development experience, and discuss one that could have been improved.
- What's in your professional portfolio?

NOTE

1. Smith (2017, p. 13).

Chapter 15

Learning Facilities

The idea of innovative learning spaces inside and outside the traditional walls of schools can contribute positively to a school culture. Changing the physical plant of a school can be incredibly costly. In some cases, such transformations require added funding, but in many cases, the costs of such changes can be minimal, or easily be shared or absorbed by local stakeholders involved in local community improvement projects.

Often neglected spaces that can support learning are gardens, signage, parking, and walkways. With a creative nudge, such spaces can become a canvas for a painted scaled version of the solar system, world maps or grounds peppered with kindness and peace gardens.

When you step into a school, the entranceway, like the beginning of a Disney attraction, can tell a story. Beyond the typical introductory scene featuring the trophy cases and sterile hallways, some schools strive to make more of an impact. In one school in DC, visitors and community members are greeted by an exhibit of forty elegantly framed 5 × 7 photographs of soon-to-be graduates. At another school, the amphibious greeter, "Sterling" the fish, captured the attention of many. Some schools herald multiple banners from colleges to promote high expectations. Being met by real images of real people, however, provides evidence that in these spaces learning and happiness do not have to be strangers.

If a school can secure $500 to $1,000 in the budget for changing up the look of the entranceway or halls at different times through the school year, it can be stimulating for students, staff and community members. School facilities can and should reflect thinking outside the box; there should be no limit to what can be done!

According to Fullan and Langworthy (2014), "there is room for debate on whether new pedagogies benefit from different types of facilities with different space arrangements than traditional classroom-based schools. Major changes to facilities design would, of course, incur additional expense" (p. 71). Changing the physical plant of the school can amount to serious expenditures. Some schools that identify with STEM and STEAM missions feature many ways of using the physical plant to enhance learning: natural Learning Spaces (butterfly sanctuaries, adventure playgrounds); outdoor Pavilions (for game play and display of nature "collections"); reference monitors/ computer screens built into tables for easy browsing, online research and checking for understanding; green room for examining the arts and Science of Music, Visual, and Digital Arts, such as photography and film/TV making; kitchens (indoor and outdoor) for exploring the Science of cooking; lunchrooms as "Energy Labs"; Pizza Garden—with ingredients to add to a pizza; observatories—exploring the changing state of stars and planets in the universe; running Tracks—built from recycled materials (i.e., running shoes); tree-houses—designing, building and maintenance; re-purposing old school buses to make a greenhouse, writer's getaway, museum, polygon factory, or a make-believe time machine; makerspaces (PBL Labs' Recycled Toy Factory, Robotics, Model Train rooms, Genius Hour, etc.); and spaces for archeological digs.

TECHNOLOGY AND SPACE

Mitra's (1999) *Hole in the Wall* Project provided some surprising findings. His research team placed a computer inside an outside wall in a slum area in Kalkaji, New Delhi, in India. He noted:

> The screen was visible from the street . . . the PC was available to anyone who passed by. The computer had online access . . . but no instructions were given for its use. What happened next astonished us. Children came running out of the nearest slum and glued themselves to the computer. They couldn't get enough. They began to click and explore. They began to learn how to use this strange thing. A few hours later, . . . the children were actually surfing the Web. (2012)

Social use of technology can be far more constructive than working in isolation on a computer.

Schools need to figure out ways to renovate classrooms with technology stations or pods for coding, robotics, gaming, quizzes, database, spreadsheet, graphing, PowerPoint, video, and web design work. Upfront funding is required to ensure proper wiring and mounts for projectors. The main costs for accessing Internet services for multiple classrooms in a school can cost as little as $100 per month, and when bundled with a landline and designated cell phone service, such costs can be less than $200 per month. While facility technology services can be reasonable, there are other facility-related expenses that can be much more expensive.

RENOVATING AND MODELLING CREATIVITY

Renovation is quite common in homes and businesses, yet the layout of many schools and classrooms tends to look much like it did a century ago. Making changes to a physical plant can be a significant investment, and as such, it should inspire learning. How can we expect students to be the inventors of tomorrow by housing them in cookie-cutter schools and classrooms today? Students do not just hear talk about being creative, they can witness it in their innovative surroundings.

School renovations should not focus on replicating the antiseptic look of a spotless condo entranceway; nor should school communities be satisfied with a few new pillars on the outside of a sporting complex. Serious thought about how each change can support learning is necessary. At one school, the Math teacher-leader painted multiples on each step in the stairwell so students could see number patterns and relationships, ideally promoting the mastery of multiplication tables for the younger learners.

In several schools, ceiling tiles at a cost of $150 per wall were used as bulletin boards. Homemade whiteboards cost roughly $100 per wall, and even less to cover student tables with whiteboard paint. Compare these prices with commercial whiteboard or cork boards that take up less space. At a cost of approximately $700, colorful educational rugs, can provide active spaces for students to move around and experience number patterns or explore the periodic table. If you think about it, every square inch of classroom space can be a canvas for learning.

It may be easy to place commercial posters in strategic spaces in classrooms, but ideally most space should be reserved for student work. When the walls are left blank, or filled up by teacher resources, there is a missed opportunity for students to connect and share their work in the classroom. When teachers put up student work, they are honoring their contributions. Students can only learn from each other, too.

OFFICE SPACE—OR NOT?

Is it possible for a school to function without multiple office spaces? The way we organized "offices" sixty years ago does not have to be the same way we use office spaces today. Tracking the demand and use of such spaces would be a good place to begin an inquiry into use of school office spaces.

What would it be like if the front office staff be moved to the entrance, no longer separated from the community by an over-sized counter? The costs for opening up spaces and removing offices can vary, but some estimates can be as low as $8000.

UPDATING SCHOOL SPACE FORMULAS

To make changes to the physical plant, it is important to have a solid understanding of minimum space requirements for schools and various classroom sizes. Policies, that define how large or small public schools will be, are largely determined at the district or state level. Different states and provinces use elaborate formulas to ensure equity, and for meeting school space and safety codes. In Ontario, the office space is regulated based on the number of students (3.1 square feet per student up to a maximum of 1,500 square feet). This space includes principal and vice principal office spaces, guidance areas, health rooms, and a secured storage area for academic records (p. 13).

The detailing of gymnasium, libraries, cafeterias, storage area, and other office spaces are included in many state and provincial regulation documents. To be prepared for new learning demands, facility and classroom space formulas need to be updated to keep up with ongoing changes in learning needs. According to the California Department of Education (2007): "Districts have built schools with basically the same funding model for the past 60 years, and it is the changing educational program that has had to adapt to the static funding model" (p. 12).

Table 15.1 outlines sample square footage data from four different jurisdictions:

It makes sense for systems to regulate space, especially when looking to ensure healthy learning conditions and equity of facility fund allocation. The

Table 15.1 Sample Square Footage Requirements for General Classroom Space

Location	Classroom Square Footage
New York	17–22 square feet/student
Ontario	750 square feet. (23–26 students)
Virginia	Pre-K, Kindergarten—975 square feet
	Grade 1 Grades 2–5—800 square feet
	Grades 6—12—700 square feet
Washington State	K-6 schools—90 square feet;
	Grades 7–8 schools—117 square feet;
	Grades 9–12 schools–130 square feet

collateral impact, however of prescribing school and classroom dimensions can serve to diminish the variety of unique schools dedicated to distinct forms of learning. Flexible standards that provide guidelines for funding a range of space options would better serve students, staff, and community members dedicated to innovative schooling.

SHARED FACILITIES

Some schools team up with community recreational programs. In this way, they can share costs for construction and maintenance of gymnasiums, pools, gardens, and fitness trails. Looking for ways to use facilities, year-round, rather than ten months a year makes good sense when thinking about shared costs for heating, air conditioning, maintenance, and a host of other physical plant necessities. In some cases, schools have provided community spaces for dental and medical healthcare, as well as banking opportunities that can serve to enrich financial literacy. Some innovative schools have built in stores, restaurants, and daycare services.

Referring to the U.K. and U.S. experiments with full-service community schools, Whitby (2018) noted: "This is a collaborative approach between education, health and community services that becomes a one stop shop for families . . . a response that aims to be effective and economical."

Grappling with Ideas

- Take some time to think about your facility use and the habits reinforced by such arrangements and use of materials. Discuss.
- What would be the advantages and disadvantages if your school evolved into a full-service community school? Share your insights.

Chapter 16

Being Small

All roads in this examination of great schools leads back to small schools, and while it may seem plausible that larger schools save money, this is a huge assumption, as there is little if any peer-reviewed research to back up such a claim. Furthermore, the goal of education is not to save money, but to build a stronger society.

There are many reasons why small schools are better than larger schools. Hylden (2005) claimed that, "a growing body of data now shows clearly that small schools, by nearly all significant measurements, outperform large schools" is backed up by the research that indicates that students perform better academically; graduate at higher levels; are more likely to attend college; earn higher salaries later on in life; participate more in extracurricular activities; have better rates of attendance; report greater positive attitudes toward learning; and, are less likely to face school-related crime and violence. Hylden (2005) also noted that teachers: report greater job satisfaction; are more likely to feel as if they are succeeding in their work; are often more able to identify problems; respond innovatively and effectively; and adapt to change.

Studies comparing results of standardized tests indicate that students from smaller schools outperform students from larger schools.[1]

Raywid (1999) determined that there is "reliable evidence of the positive effects of small school size on student success," as well as, the "devastating effects of large size on substantial numbers of youngsters" (p. 3). Being deliberately small can enhance a sense of community within and beyond the school walls. "Neighborhoods in which small towns are found," according to Hylden, provide "a central meeting place and source of activity, building community ties and relationships, enhancing the democratic process through mutual goal-setting and decision-making, providing added economic activity, and acting as a source for community pride and identity."

Supporters of large schools often lose sight of the ideal safety conditions in small schools. According to Grauer and Ryan (2018): "students in smaller schools fight less, feel safer, come to school more frequently, and report being more attached to their school." Their view that: "It is impossible to dismiss school size as a powerful and fundamental indicator of safety" is difficult to refute. The social dynamics are significantly different in schools where you can feel anonymous.

According to Nathan and Thao (2001): "Students at large schools are more prone to be alienated from their peers." Colleges and universities tend to have students on larger campuses, and while sometimes they are broken down into smaller groupings in specific faculties, it can be challenging for students in large universities to feel a sense of community. Does it make sense to have "superschools"? Larmer (2018) was concerned Marjory Stoneman Douglas High School had over 3000 students and Columbine High School in 1999 had almost 2000 students.

> The shooters in these places were alienated young men. In schools of that size, how many students are well known by the adults there? Not many. How can teachers know and care for their students when they might see 150 or more a day in five or six classes on a 50-minute bell schedule? They can't. The size and structure of the factory-model high school is part of the problem.

Apart from the accumulated research on the value of small schools, decision-makers in education would be well advised to read the assembled material about small schools on the *Community Work Institute.org* website. Perhaps, such understandings might help reverse, or slow down, the trend in many districts of building new "superschools," while shutting down smaller ones. School expenses, large or small, are profoundly tied to human capital, and to date; no funds are saved by closing small schools. According to Grauer (2018), while some research is scattered and unreliable, there are findings that reveal that: "larger schools with enrollments in excess of 1200 have not produced expected economies of scale that result in better lower per-pupil costs when compared to true small schools" (p. 7).

If exceptional teaching is central to learning, then a school leader needs to be able to know how each staff member is improving. The larger the number of students, the larger the leadership team needed to manage the span of control. These kinds of costs are rarely calculated by people who see large schools as a source of savings; and, when decision-makers increase the span of control beyond ten people, then the quality of teaching can be at risk.

As the number of pupils increase, so do the numbers of highest paid staff needed to provide oversight of students and staff. For instance, "superschools" do not save money by having fewer vice principals; in fact, some of these schools budget for upwards of five VPs. In the same vein, more guidance counselors, special education staff, and custodians are needed to address the larger footprint of the school. Students still require classrooms with ideal teacher: student ratios; so long as the number of students increase, so will the need to staff a school to meet their needs. The notion that "superschools" save taxpayer dollars is a myth.

Research from Slate and Jones (2005) confirms that: "Increasing school size, especially beyond 400 students, does not typically result in a large increase in curricular offerings." When school leaders work creatively to staff schools and build schedules, students in small schools have the potential to reap comparable curricular benefits. According to Grauer (2018), "an exhaustive course and club catalog is not fundamental as a determinant of excellent schooling, nor is it a proven way to accommodate diverse student tastes and interests" (p. 7).

When comparing the fiscal costs of small and large schools, it is rare to read about costs associated with: increased dropout rates in large schools; increased violence in large schools; decreased sense of social safety and connectedness in large schools; lower teacher satisfaction and higher teacher turnover in large schools; lower achievement in college from students in large schools; and, less happiness of students in large schools.

Yet, these realities come with significant costs to society. Given that these are not fixed costs, they are rarely considered in comparative calculations that simplify things, such as the difference in volume of heated spaces. Many formulas for convincing school boards to shut down smaller schools "tend to disguise tremendous noncash costs associated closely with large schools."[2]

Given that schooling can affect a nation's productivity, it becomes important to debate whether large or small schools matter.

Grappling with Ideas

- How can you put a price tag on a schools' influence on community growth or higher future incomes?
- How can the long-term costs of ignoring mental health needs come without social-economic costs?

Discuss Dr. Brooks's question:

- Why do we keep the focus on building gigantic schools when we now have over 30 years of promising small schools' data?

NOTES

1. Bryk and Driscoll (1988), Gladden (2000), Howley, Strange and Bickel (2000), Husbands and Beese (2004), Lee and Smith (1997), Raywid (1980).
2. Grauer (2018).

Part 3

HOW CAN WE AFFORD CHANGE?

Without a struggle, there can be no progress

—Frederick Douglass

HOW CAN WE AFFORD CHANGE?

The school budget represents an important force in making significant change in schools happen, or not. When budgets can change and funds can be re-purposed, a school can move beyond the "sameness" struggle to reach greatness. Decision-makers should not be in the dark about school budgets. They should understand how budgets and financial statements can be broken down into various expense categories, and they should know how to break down expenses within each category according to specific line item costs. On the one hand, it can be helpful to view other budgets, but moving beyond a budget struggle in schools involves understanding how grants, other sources of revenue, cost savings, and re-purposing budgets can contribute to, and support, change.

There is no point in discussing greatness and innovation in schools without knowing if such changes are affordable. Schools cannot target improvement without adjustments being made to their budgets. Being great is much more than adopting a cookie-cutter budget that reveals a cookie-cutter vision that is grounded in cookie-cutter values. By shifting the economies of schools, it is possible to move further toward greatness.

Chapter 17

Inside School Budgets

This chapter does not reveal one ideal budget; rather, it highlights details of financial statements from two independent schools, one charter high school and another elementary charter school. By examining these four school budgets, it was possible to identify four "expenditure categories" that classify line items on budgets that address key needs of a school. The names of each school and their locations were not disclosed; rather, the pseudonyms, School A, B, C, and D, were used for identification purposes.

While common features were apparent among the varied financial statements, each school addressed their budgets in different ways. These schools have different purposes, serve different populations, and span diverse regions across North America; as such, each budget is unique.

A review of the line items in each of the four sample budgets reveal some common features that include the funding for human capital and other ways schools spend portions of their budgets. Seeing a variety of budget options can provide alternative perspectives when planning for new or transforming schools. Having been involved in three school start-ups, one thing is certain: no matter how much you plan for your expenses, there will be surprises. The unintended purchase of a sprinkler system or a septic tank can divert funds in an instance.

Absent from these samplings are traditional public school budgets, auxiliary central office budgets, or budgets of large "superschools." It is possible, however, to compare expenses and revenues for any school, as there are many common elements among budgets. For the most part, investment in human capital continues to take up the critical mass of expenditures, while what remains seems to be parceled out in predictable chunks afforded to textbooks, classroom materials, and various physical plant and other operational costs. The following financial statements provide four school examples for refection and examination of patterns and distinguishing features of school budgets (table 17.1).

School A: This sample budget was developed for a new charter high school that opened with 120 students. The Math and ELA teachers also had special education qualifications.

School B: Table 17.2 outlines a K-12 independent school budget that supports 210 students in a tuition-based school that has a combination of certified teachers and community-based noncertified itinerant teachers with distinct local talents (Table 17.3).

School C: This K-8 independent inquiry-based school has twenty-four students with seven staff members.

School D: Table 17.4 highlights a K-8 charter school with over 70 staff members and 400 students.

Table 17.1 School "A" Financial Statement (new charter high school)

School A Financial Statement	
Revenue	
Federal Sources	265,000.00
State Sources	870,000.00
Local Sources	540,0000.00
Total Revenue	1,675,000.00
Instruction (Teachers, Supplies, etc.)	433,185.00
Pupil Support Services	1800.00
Instructional Staff Services (Improvement of Instruction, Technology, and Academic Student Assessment)	145,675.00
General Administrative Services (Board Legal, Authorizer Fee, management company fees)	262,000.00
School Administration Services (Principal, Assistant Principal, office staff, supplies, etc.)	121,880.00
Business Services (Financial Management, Due and Fees, Interest, and Insurance)	52,200.00
Food Services	73,300.00
Operations and Maintenance (Facility Maintenances Security Insurance, Utilities and Rent)	212,100.00
Pupil Transportation Services	1950.00
Central Services (Communication, Staff/Personnel/HR, IT Support and Pupil Accounting)	85,800.00
Capital Outlay (New Classroom depreciable equipment/furniture; Land and Building Improvement	331,000.00
Payment on Capital Leases, Principal and Interest on Long-Term Equipment Financing	55,500.00
Total Expenditures	1,776,390.00
Balance	(-101,390.000)

Inside School Budgets 89

Table 17.2 School "B" Financial Statement (K-12 independent school)

School B Financial Statement	
Tuition	4,760,000.00
Grants and Student Aid	2,340,000.00
Fees (Application, Technology, Bus, Supplies)	231,100.00
Endowment Interest	16,000.00
Bus Fees	85,000.00
Rent Revenue	32,000.00
Donations and Fundraising	50,000.00
Total Revenue	7,429,100.00
Accounting Expense	30,000.00
Advertising Expense	25,000.00
Bank Charges	11,100.00
GST Paid	10,000.00
Insurance Expense	30,000.00
Meeting Expense	2,000.00
Office Materials and Supplies	50,000.00
Office Equipment (Leases)	41,000.00
Rent	360,000.00
Custodial Expenses	95,000.00
Repairs and Maintenance	40,000.00
Staff Fund	6,000.00
Telephone and Utilities	53,000.00
Teaching Salaries	4,700,000.00
Substitute Teachers	5,000.00
Itinerant Teachers	15,000.00
Benefits (EI, CPP Expense, WCB, MSP, Extended Health, LTD, RRSP, Vacation Pay)	747,600.00
Payroll Expense	9,900.00
Busing Costs	90,000.00
Field Trips	55,000.00
Total Technology (Repairs, Equipment, Support)	81,500.00
Curriculum Support	30,000.00
Library	5,000.00
Miscellaneous Student Expenses	30,000.00
Professional Development	30,000.00
Sports Equipment	2,000.00
Total Student Services (Psychologist, Speech, OT, Counseling, Consultants)	454,000.00
Pro-rated/Discounted Tuition	125,000.00
Student Materials and Supplies	55,000.00
Textbooks	4,000.00
Uniform Costs	7,000.00
Contingency	50,000.00
Total Expense	7,249,100.00
Balance	180,000.00

Table 17.3 School "C" Financial Statement (K-8 independent school)

School C Financial Statement	
Revenue	341,120.00
Tuition	298,920.00
Afterschool Program	36,000.00
Application Fees	1200.00
Summer Camps	5000.00
Expenses	338,490.00
Payroll Total (including Workman's Comp; Taxes)	241,000.00
• Teacher 1	70,000.00
• Teacher 2	70,000.00
• Assistant 1	15,000.00
• Assistant 2	15,000.00
• Office Assistant	15,000.00
• Director	40,000.00
• Afterschool Leader	15,000.00
• Substitute Teachers	1,000.00
Computer Subscriptions	600.00
Classroom Materials	8,800.00
Activities/PE	4,000.00
Furniture Replacement	1,000.00
Music	4,000.00
Assessments	2,000.00
Tech support	300.00
Electric, Gas	2,040.00
Water	360.00
Rent	50,400.00
CEU (Professional Development)	2,000.00
Cleaning	5,760.00
Security	300.00
Internet/Phone	2,280.00
Tax Return	50.00
Bus Insurance	2,000.00
Bus Maintenance	1,000.00
Professional Liability Insurance	4,900.00
Web Security	200.00
After School Programming	3,200.00
File Monitoring	300.00
Gifts/Dinners	2,000.00
Balance	2,630.00

Table 17.4 School "D" Financial Statement (K-8 Charter School)

School D Financial Statement	
Revenues	7,885,000.00
Per Pupil Charter Payments (440 students)	5,558,000.00
Per Pupil Summer School	460,000.00
Per Pupil Facilities Allowance	1,300,000.00
Government Funding/Grants	490,000.00
Private Grants and Donations	17,000.00
Activity Fees	60,000.00
Expenses	7,378,000.00
Principal/Executive	220,000.00
Teachers	1,600,000.00
Special Education	300,000.00
Summer School	55,000.00
Teacher Aides/Assistants	300,000.00
Before/After Care	60,000.00
Business/Operations	285,000.00
Custodial	140,000.00
Employee Benefits and Taxes	575,000.00
Other Staff and Contracted Staff; Other Educational Professionals	275,000.00
Community Guest Instructors	325,000.00
Staff Development Expense	100,000.00
Textbooks	50,000.00
Student Supplies and Materials and Student Expenses	129,000.00
Library and Media Center Materials and Computers	57,000.00
Student Assessment Materials	30,000.00
Contracted Student Services	350,000.00
Transportation	5,000.00
Food Service	370,000.00
Rent (and Depreciation Expense—37.000)	1,237,000.00
Utilities	112,500.00
Building Maintenance, Repairs and Renovations (Leasehold Improvements)	105,000.00
Classroom and office Furnishings and Supplies and Equipment	20,000.00
Telephone/Telecommunications	62,500.00
Janitorial Supplies (25,000) + Contracted Building Services (95,000)	120,000.00
Office Supplies and Materials; Postage and Shipping; Printing and Copying	86,000.00
Office Equipment Rental and Maintenance	10,000.00
Legal, Accounting, and Payroll Services	185,000.00
Insurance	63,000.00
Administration Fee to Authorizer	37,000.00
Interest Expense (67,000) and Other General Expense (47,000)	114,000.00
Balance	507,000.00

Analysis: Without being part of each school, it is difficult to compare these distinct budgets, especially when different line items featured some varying terms. As I viewed each budget, I made a master list of questions specific to the actual spending in each budget:

1. What does this budget directly spend on students?
2. What percentage of the school budget is dedicated to human capital?
3. What percentage of the budget contracts services outside the school?
4. How much of the school budget is committed to professionalism and staff development?
5. How do facility, maintenance, and utility costs affect the overall budget?
6. How well are safety and security costs delineated in this budget?
7. What percentage of the overall budget is dedicated to administrative costs?

These questions served as the basis for collapsing themes from which to view each budget through a common lens or domain:

- Staffing (and Contracted Services/Products) and Staff Development
- Direct Spending on Students (materials; technology; food; transportation)
- Facilities, Utilities, and Security
- Administrative Costs (office supplies; promotion)

As well, questions about sustainability emerged when viewing the balance and financial details. Budgets with larger balances did appear to be more sustainable, and less vulnerable, and therefore, ideally prepared for contingency plans, if necessary. Also, it was easier to analyze more transparent financial statements that had more line items, and less general categories. In such cases of fewer items, the analysis was less precise.

The variations in budgets illustrate that they do not need to be fixed; rather, there are ample ways to revise spending to adjust for new or changing values in a school. Given that the budget revenues range from approximately $220,000 to $8 million in U.S. currency, the costs vary in terms of actual expenditures. There were also some variations in terms of the percentage of the total costs spent on certain areas of the budgets. Table 17.5 illustrates how each budget expense was broken down (using percentages and sum totals) to further examine patterns for further discussion.

From a first glance of the "staffing" and "contracted services," category, it is evident that education is a labor-intensive operation. In schools, human capital can be spread between staff with benefits and contract workers without benefits. In all cases, human capital expenditures took up a healthy portion of the school budgets.

Table 17.5 Breakdown of Expenditures Categories in Four School Budgets

Expenditure Categories	Budget A	Budget B	Budget C	Budget D
Staffing Costs	555,065.00 (~31%)	5,542,600 (~76%)	240,000.00 (~71%)	3,535,000.00 (~48%)
• Contracted Services	547,475.00 (~31%)	596,900.00 (~8%)	1,050.00 (<1%)	1,330,000.00 (~18%)
• Professionalism and Staff Development		68,000.00 (<1%)	4,000.00 (~1%)	100,000.00 (~1%)
Direct Student Impact Expenditures	75,250.00 (~4%)	454,500.00 (~6)	25,900.00 (~8%)	641,000.00 (9%)
Facility, Utilities, and Security	542,100.00 (~30%)	580,000.00 (~8%)	60,560.00 (~18%)	1,474,500.00 (~20%)
Administrative Costs	55,500.00 (~3%)	165,100.00 (~2%)	2,580.00 (<1%)	297,500.00 (~4%)

STAFFING AND CONTRACT SERVICES

Wages can vary from school to school or district to district, depending on negotiated agreements, or in some cases, a price demand. Everyone can learn that change at the school level usually requires a change at the budget level. Given that improvement does not happen in a vacuum, that is, without change, it follows that values can shape the forces of change that can transform school cultures. In conventional public schools, the pay grid is published in an agreement and/or an employee handbook. In charter schools such grids do not seem to be commonplace; there does not seem to be systematic ways of paying staff fairly.

The range of salary proportions of the total budget may have more to do with the degree to which schools opt to outsource different kinds of services. For instance, schools can save money on benefits when they contract out some special education services, before and after programs, security, payroll, and often, to a partial extent, janitorial work. The proportion of nonteaching staff to teaching staff in schools can vary, as well.

In the United States, the number of disability cases has risen from 1 in 184 in 1987, to 1 in 76 in 2007. "For children, the rise is even more startling—a thirty-five-fold increase in the same two decades."[1] Special education teachers and school administrators often have exceptional teaching backgrounds, yet their typical roles tend to separate them from the classroom. Hiring more teachers with special education qualifications can help increase the ongoing supports in classrooms, at the same time as reducing the overall teacher: student ratios.

Some schools may contract services. They may hire fewer custodians who work in the day, but contract a janitorial company during the evening and/or on weekends to do "deep cleans" when students and staff are not present.

It is also popular for schools to hire full-time in-house "coaches" to support developing teachers, but this takes talent out of the direct reach of students, who miss out on having "coaches" as their teachers. The notion of half-time coaches or mentors, who also have a half-time teaching load, can provide ideal opportunities for both students and colleagues. Depending on the needs of the school, consulting companies may be contracted to provide staff supports; however, this can run counter to more progressive schools that develop teacher-leader talent from within.

Wooster (2018) shared his skepticism about one turn-around consulting group in DC. He noted that charter schools should be different than one another and was skeptical of consulting firms that pushed all schools "to offer the same classes taught in the same ways" (p. 5). Wooster (2018) was also concerned about consulting teams being paid over $100,000 a month while "leaving teaching positions vacant" (p. 4). Transparency around payments to consulting companies would help educators understand more clearly how much of the public trough is, or is not, being depleted.

The use of public funds to turn schools around may seem like the right thing to do; however, it should require much more finesse than examining a simple compilation of easy metrics (test scores and attendance). Rather than taking the time and putting in the hard work to help people re-shape and improve their school cultures, many so-called "experts" try to fast-track short-term results to prove that charter schools are better options. Given that human capital carves up so much of the school budget, it makes sense to look beyond the quick fixes to how restructuring can save schools money and re-direct expenses, so they have a direct impact on students and staff development.

Finally, the percentage of funds dedicated to PD tend to be far behind the "administrative costs" in most schools, If teachers are so critical to student learning, why is this investment in their development so low in many schools? Less than 1% of any budget for PD—just doesn't cut it.

DIRECT STUDENT IMPACT EXPENDITURES

Schools should spend more money directly on students. Students should be provided with learning materials of the print and digital kind. Often there are considerable funds allocated for testing materials. While the breakdown of many student costs can be afforded to transportation and food services, it makes sense to look at how monies are directed more to learning (beyond testing), than the narrow investment in feeding and transporting these key stakeholders to and from school.

Institutions developed for students should direct a higher percentage of the revenue to them, than what is currently afforded in schools. Without changes to the areas of the budget that incur the greatest expenses, it is difficult to increase the direct student impact of schools on students.

FACILITY, UTILITIES, AND SECURITY

How much a school invests in the facility, utilities, and security can be costly. While these expenses only attributed to approximately 8% of School B's budget, School A's budget had to withstand an enormous depletion to cover such costs from their revenue base. With so many empty schools, I often wonder why the facility rental or purchase costs remain so high. It makes it difficult for schools with high facility, maintenance, and utility expenses to have much to pay teachers and cover student needs. Getting such costs down under 15% would be a viable goal for retaining more direct funding for students, salaries, and staff development.

The maintenance costs of different facilities are distinct in each school. Certain renovations may be scheduled for five and ten-year cycles, making it difficult to compare the needs of different physical plants. Whether schools opt for air conditioning can also be an expensive, but necessary, health consideration.

Often safety and security costs are embedded in staffing and facility costs as schools may outsource these services to professional agencies. The initial purchase of security cameras, locks, and scanners, for instance, represent key items in capital budgets, but many security-related items require ongoing maintenance. With more recent concerns surrounding school shootings, it is anticipated that this area of the budget may continue to increase. School C listed web security as a line item cost, and given the rise in social media bullying, and the need to protect privacy, schools will need to be vigilant about oversight and ready to budget for these costs, in addition to providing increasing oversight.

ADMINISTRATIVE COSTS

It was a relief to see such low administrative costs across the board in each of the sample school budgets. Many administrative costs, however, can be hidden in contract services, so viewing the budget, line-by-line, can help interpret whether too much is being spent on certain operational expenses.

BUDGETARY LENSES

Budgets can be viewed through three lenses: sustainability, transparency, and materiality.

Sustainability

The notion of sustainability in the short term can be illuminated by the revenue generated, the balance sheet, and whether financing is required to keep the ship afloat. Financial Statement B included the allocation of $50,000 for possible contingency needs when unexpected expenses arise after budget approval. It's important for schools to minimize a false sense of financial security. Being too reliant on free goods and services increases a school's vulnerability, and therefore, challenges its' long-term sustainability.

Relying on government allocations for publicly funded schools will probably not be enough to build a great school culture. Schools can generate additional revenue, or look for cost-saving ways to re-purpose existing funds to support new initiatives. When the critical mass of a staff can accept the challenge of finding new ways to carve up the budget, a culture of innovation can emerge. Without change, it is difficult to sustain anything.

Transparency

Transparency in a budget, for this analysis, refers to the capacity of the reader to understand what is meant by each line item. It was surprising to view such clarity in many of these budgets. There were two budgets, however that used terms such as "contracted student services"; "other staff and contracted staff, other educational professionals"; "general/ executive administrative services"; "school administration services"; "business services"; "operations and maintenance"; "central services"; and "other financing sources" which did not delineate how precisely money was spent.

A budget needs to clearly indicate how much is being spent on outside consultants and an examination of the fiscal benefits that can accompany the process of re-staffing a school. As noted:

> Consultant groups are making a pretty penny for reforming/reorganizing schools. <one> group . . . was charging us $200/hour just for reading resumes! These companies can charge upwards of $200,000 per year for auditing a school, recommending their own on-site need to fix it, and then re-stocking it with new staff . . . such payments are bundled into "general" administrative cost categories, and remain hidden from public viewing.[2]

Transparency can build stakeholder trust when you can see how the numbers add up.

When schools do not have pay grids, or when budgets are padded or lined with uncertain line items, it is possible for staff and community members to question the integrity of how money is spent. In public institutions, budgets should be transparent; after all, taxes are funding these schools. Independent schools, with nonprofit status, should also make their budgets transparent, so they have ample evidence reflecting that revenues are diverted toward necessary school expenses. In the case of private schools, there are no legal obligations to share budgetary choices; the stakeholder essentially must trust, without verification, that the owners of such schools are acting in the best interest of the students.

Materiality

These sample budgets clearly indicate that staffing, as well as facility costs are the most "material" categories in a school budget. The costs of operating a school more efficiently, would require decision-makers to tackle such items, as together they average more than 79% of the total budget. Notably, less than 1% of the budgets are dedicated to professional development, which reveals that such items are less valued. While professional development may be hidden within other costs, as a line item in these budgets, it appears to be immaterial. It would be preferential to view larger school samples and more financial statements over the course of several years, to establish more accurate trends in how each expenditure category, namely: staffing, student-directed expenses, facilities, and administrative costs, meet the tests of sustainability, transparency and materiality.

Grappling with Ideas

- How can shifting job responsibilities free up more funds in a school?
- How transparent are the budgets that you work within?
- What are the most material expenditure categories in your budget and how can they be revised to support school improvement?
- What is the overall percentage of your budget for staff development?

NOTES

1. Angell (2011).
2. Smith (2016).

Chapter 18

Saving Money and Generating Revenue

The budget needs to reflect how change can happen in schools. Depending on the nature of the innovation, schools can acquire grants, generate new sources of revenue, implement cost-saving measures, and re-allocate funds to support school change and improvement.

GRANTS

In a perfect world, the ideal school would be designed with the descriptions of the basic funding needs, as well as the identification of additional costs associated with enhancing and sustaining specific programming, or operating needs of the school. Businesses and foundations that develop grants try to anticipate various needs of schools, and therefore, provide substantive funding for targeted supports (see appendices A and B).

There were some key grants issued in the United States between 2010 and 2015 by the U.S. Department of Education. Sornson (2017b) noted that more than $7 billion in *School Improvement Grants* (SIG's) were awarded to reform some 5,000 struggling or "failing" schools. Some grants can drive innovation, but they can also stifle opportunities at the same time. To ensure equity, there are often requirements that short-term data reveal that the funded project is having a significant impact, immediately. After all, if something appears to not be working, another project might be more deserving of the funding. The dilemma arises when the "sameness" of grant applications gives rise to quick fix actions that spin their own bureaucracy, which then requires more human capital to manage the project at both ends: the school and the foundation.

Grants are tools that can drive and limit innovation at the same time. For instance, it is rare for the criterion and process for funding expectations to undergo scrutiny. While grants need to ensure accountability, ideally, they should model the kinds of innovation they are hoping to promote. For instance, how often do grants ask for satisfaction surveys or evidence of student learning beyond test scores?

GENERATING REVENUE

Beyond the grant process, there are some schools that generate funds by making goods and services available to their local or greater communities. Some schools can be quite creative in their efforts to generate revenue. Pepper (2018) shared how students at the Lakewood Ranch High School in Bradenton, Florida raised money by organizing an auto show. The event featured close to one hundred classic cars. Local car dealerships and accessory stores paid a fee to set up booths, and overall, the school banked about $3000.

Schools can generate revenue by creating their own thrift shops, sports equipment trade-in centers, or by using space to house a local museum. Students, staff, and families can donate the sale of their art work, and some schools have entered talent in the *America's Got Talent* competition in search of $1,000,000! Some schools have opened daycares, while others have provided parking and auto cleaning services on a regular basis.

Schools can rent out space to the local community on weekends, holidays, or during the school day, provided safety plans are in place. Some schools have generated funds through *Kickstarter* and *DonorsChoose* campaigns. Young inventors can donate their proceeds, or portions of their proceeds, back to the school that housed, guided, and supported the development of their various innovations.

SAVING MONEY

There are many ways to save money in schools. Installing solar panels can reduce utility costs over the long term, and as prices continue to drop for panels, the conversation about solar energy in schools should move from the textbook to the budget room. Purchasing automatic soap dispensers for bathrooms can save on ongoing soap expenses. Some schools have intelligent lighting that is only on when people are in the classroom. Looking at the details carefully can help generate ideas for cost savings.

As difficult as it is to ask for help, whether in the form of money, goods, or deeds, it can make a difference in the quest for school greatness. It wasn't easy over the years asking friends, colleagues, and strangers for support, but with all that was needed to open new schools, a coordinated effort made, what seemed like the impossible, possible. A school leader should be proud of his or her school, willing to go the extra mile, and willing to stand on a pulpit and bring others on board to believe and support the mission. The more hands chipping in, the more money saved, and with less wasted funding, there is more budget that can be dedicated toward meeting student and staff needs.

More savings are possible when schools consider reducing excessive transportation costs. If students can make it to the school via public transport or parent drop offs, there are considerable savings to be had. The cost of fuel makes it difficult to project these kinds of expenses. Even when a bus company is contracted to do this work, the school needs an adult on board to supervise the safety of all students. The human capital expenses associated with having responsible adults on board every bus can be significant. Furthermore, over and above the regular insurance premiums, there are additional fees afforded for covering the risk of transporting students. Schools may own their own bus and, as such, are required to ensure that the drivers are certified and that the bus is maintained.

The provision, or not, of a food services program can also be a costly endeavor for a school. The idea of having lunch prepared for the masses may seem like a wonderful convenience, but it can be an expensive option for a school. If students and staff can bring their own food, it saves on staffing and often food waste. In some cases, kitchens can enhance a school mission especially when students can learn culinary skills, and perhaps establish a food industry that could generate additional revenue to cover the costs associated with such programs.

REPURPOSING EXISTING BUDGETS

There are many ways to repurpose existing line-items in budgets. When a school can adjust staff roles, it is possible to make room in the budget to increase staff or save funds for other purposes. Given that staffing payments represent the largest proportion of expenditures in a school budget, it is important to think creatively about restructuring staff positions to increase efficiency and reduce duplication of work. It is also possible to revise other expenditures in the budget, such as facilities and staff development, and to look more closely at resource allocation. To make room for change, whether facilitated by the addition of new staff members or the need to purchase new materials, a budget will need to be adjusted; school leaders will need to take funds that are typically dedicated to certain areas and reduce them. The idea of moving budgets away from fixed line items is necessary for change, but nevertheless challenging to implement.

In one high school, we hired Math and ELA teachers who were also qualified in Special Education. We made sure that their classes had no more than ten students in them, so that students who required small group settings to support their Individual Education Plans (IEP's) would have help for two hours a day within these key subject areas. Rather than have Special Education teachers follow another teacher's curriculum, they were responsible for teaching and ensuring all their students were learning. By having two teachers with duo-qualifications, we could keep the teacher: student ratio in these key classes to 10:1.

In a start-up school, we did not have the budget to afford to pay a Visual Arts teacher in the first year. One of our parents was a local artist who dedicated time to give students quality instruction for a small stipend. On the one hand, some schools can budget over $50,000 for a certified Visual Arts teacher, yet on the other hand, there may be talent who would volunteer or work for a stipend that could range from $1000 to $10,000.

Volunteers can add incredible depth to school programming. Some volunteers have teaching credentials and some do not. The work to ensure that such talents have been vetted for safety is well worth it. In one school, we had two parents who shared a depth and breadth of experience in the film and television industry. While we had a teacher present during the Film Studies elective, it was the parents who planned and coordinated a first-class Media Arts experience for the students. Students in grades 3, 4, and 5 had the opportunity to plan and direct their own movies. They went on to win the grand prize in a nation-wide anti-bullying video contest. While volunteering to make money for a school is commonplace, it is rare to invite parents into the teaching community.

Volunteers can contribute to a school in many ways. Parents and students can answer telephones, which can build in breaks for support staff. It can be very helpful when parents with strong technology backgrounds are willing to provide advice and support. Another volunteer helped us creates a customized software program to house the school's online report card.

Probably the most important leadership lesson is to ask for help. Whether a nonprofit donates space for a meeting or sourdough bread for a social event, the act of asking, engages the community, and saves precious costs. When decision-makers in schools look for ways to improve schools, economics comes into play. How schools deal with scarcity can be key to success and ongoing improvement. Many schools have access to grants. Staff members can be creative about generating revenue, can re-purpose their current budgets, and be aggressive about saving costs.

When values adjust, the budget needs to adjust, as well. It takes less courage to apply for grants than to figure out ways to save costs and generate revenue, but adjustments to the budget cannot be avoided. The budget can drive change, but the will to embrace change is at the heart of sustainable improvement.

Grappling with Ideas

- Do you think it's a good idea for teachers to be given additional time to write grants for the school?
- Is it worth the investment in a professional grant writer, or is it worthwhile for staff, trustees, or students to be involved in a grant writing process? Discuss.
- Why do think budgets need to adjust for innovation?

Part 4

PREPARING FOR ANYTHING

Don't prepare students for something. Prepare them for anything.

@E_Sheninger

PREPARING FOR ANYTHING

Preparing for Anything is a collection of new possibilities for school reform, innovation, and greatness. This book concluded with ideas that hopefully will prompt educators to think beyond the obvious and imagine new beginnings or transforming opportunities for embracing greatness in schools.

Plenty of talk exists about building ideal schools with the purpose of replicating existing models. There is no shortage of consultants waving standard programs in the air, driven by standard budgets, that are touted as "the" utopian solution to problems in today's schools. It is less common, however, to build a budget from a quality program out. Imagine if we designed a New School to prepare young people for anything. What if we discovered it was possible to be great with the same funding allotment, or less? There are risks that come with innovation, especially, when there is usually a need to shift dollars to address different priorities.

Chapter 19

Imagine If...

> Advances in education do not come from imitation; they come from innovation!
>
> —Thomas Gutsky

Imitation, as Gutsky (2017) suggests, does not lead to advancement of education. There are some systems that are so tightly bound by "sameness," they require a disruptive force to make room for new ideas. In other schools, foundations have been put in place that leave the door open for innovation. This chapter is a collection of ideas leading with outliers that hopefully, inspire more educators to not only paint the schoolhouse with any color, but have permission to do so, outside the lines.

This *Imagine If* chapter shares a new school story through the lens of greatness that is informed by inside voices, conditions for innovation, and the strategic revision of line items adjusted to address four school expenditure categories. A New School Story was written to help all stakeholders help students *be prepared for anything*. This is the beginning of a New School Story, not to be confused with THE new school. These ideas in no way should be interpreted as THE answer, THE solution, or THE fix for problems in today's schools; rather, this story is a collection and a synthesis of affordable possibilities.

A NEW SCHOOL STORY

At New School, it was not enough to make the mission matter. New School developed a clear vision, not aiming to perfect a fixed mission. What emerged was a school fiercely focused on implementing strategic plans that cultivated a great school defined by *inspired learning and responsible actions within an inclusive culture.*

Imagine ...

Imagine a K-12 school, deliberately small, with enrollment numbers capped at 160 students. Now think about a school being organized in multi-age groupings with class sizes not exceeding 20 students. In the primary (Grades K to 2) and junior (Grades 3–5) section of the school, there are two co-educational classes. In the Middle Prep School (Grades 6–8) and Junior High (Grades 9 and 10), there are four single-gender classes. In the Senior School (Grades 11 and 12), there are two co-ed classrooms.

Programming is organized into three semesters: Fall (September–December); Winter (January–March); and Spring (April–June), with 1 week breaks built into November, December, January, and April. For many schools, 2 weeks off for winter break is common, as well as a spring break in March or April. At New School, students and staff also have the full week of U.S. Thanksgiving, as a break within the longest semester. The predicable school calendar is organized deliberately to reduce disruption and enhance routine.

FIRST DAY OF SCHOOL

New School begins after the summer break—on the Tuesday following Labor Day. New School is close to your home. There is no need for school bus transportation. You could bike, but today you chose to walk.

When you arrive on site, you see evidence of community values. To the left of the one-story chalet-styled building is a "kindness garden" prepared by the Primary students with the help of the Junior STEM (botany) class, who have planted milkweed to build a butterfly sanctuary. There is a bike rack on the other side that is used by both adults and young people; it is brightly painted with safety reminders about wearing helmets and messages about "being fit." A homemade track, made of recycled plastic and old running shoes, surrounds a sports field; the left side of the building is braced by a climbing wall, filled with motivational messages about persistence and hard work; the playground, designed by former students, is filled with healthy active kids; fitness trails are scattered in the woodlot around the perimeter; campfire logs form circles for outdoor classroom seating; an outdoor theater, designed and built by middle or high school-aged students, salutes the arts; an outdoor oven is well-placed for cooking classes and special events; goats roam the fields cutting grass. A series of bat houses are placed in the side of the barn that is surrounded on two sides by a healthy supply of bee boxes. The sidewalks, filled with images of planets in the solar system, are framed by benches and picnic tables welcoming the community to this vibrant place of learning, dedicated not just for young people, but learners of all ages.

Today, there is a teacher band playing at the entrance. Once a week there will be some musical, dance, or athletic performances ushering us into school! You get an immediate sense that it matters for people to feel welcome, that they belong here. *Upon entry*, you see a large school sign surrounded by a wall with handprints and photographs of each student in the school. One thing is for certain: the entry area is like none other; it captures the essence and ideals of both the mission and vision. Without words, it shouts, *"this is where we are, and this is where we are going."* The clarity is refreshing, and the space large enough to house a whole school gathering, the office staff, a refurbished piano, and comfortable seating along the sides of the space.

There are no doors into a school office or high counters keeping students, parents, and staff members in their place, separate from administration. Instead, you see two rooms off the entranceway, the smaller one used as a place for quiet conversations, and the other space, called an Inspiration Room, large enough to house staff meetings, parent meetings, student council meetings, and small community meetings. On the door, there are photographs of the former graduates.

After giving the school leader a "high five," at the door, you are greeted by a brightly painted mural highlighting the themes of each Community Works class (Be Kind; Be Caring; Be a Friend; Be Courteous; Be Brave; Be a Good Sport; Be a Good Citizen; Be a Cooperative; Be a Team Player; Be Responsible; Be Resilient; Be Empathetic; Be Adventurous; Be Fun; Be a Leader; and Be You). A warm team of enthusiastic staff check you in to your program of study. By 9 a.m., all students gather in their sections at the outside campfire circle (weather permitting) or in the oversized entranceway. They sing the national anthem with pride, pledge allegiance to the flag (in the United States), recite a spirited "commitment to making a difference in the world," listen to a few inspiring words from a school leader, and then take note of key announcements. At New School, the principal has prepared messages that either link with the day in history, or address a significant current event. The principal invites feedback from students about how the message of the day connects to their own experiences.

A DAY IN THE LIFE OF A K-5 STUDENT AT NEW SCHOOL

Following the brief opening ceremony, the Primary and Junior students move to their Community Works class where they learn about making a difference in the world through character education, service learning, and health education. This curriculum is integrated with reading, writing, speaking, listening, and attention to media arts which complements the teachings in ELA. This time is also dedicated to classroom discussions, peer teacher preparation, and advisory support of the goal setting, and "getting" kind. By 10 a.m., the students head out for recess and free play. After 15–20 minutes, everyone has an energy snack before beginning their 90-minute concentrated Liberal Arts or STEM classes.

The Liberal Arts or "Imagination Class" consists of activities focused on specific Language Arts, Social Studies, and Visual Arts learning centers. This integrated course cycles students through stations where they work independently and engage in mini-lessons with their teacher. In this way, the teacher provides individualized programming for each student. There is no teacher desk; there are tables large enough for the teacher and at least two students to work at a time.

The station activities are a mix of challenges: the drama center invites social interaction, with access to wardrobe of costumes and props; the mini library, a time to explore books; the games center, a place to use rules and apply problem-solving strategies; the painting, drawing, sculpting "Center for the Arts," a mapping center where students learn to draw maps and study the world, past and present; a museum that houses artifacts that share the history of the school and the community; and a hands-on whiteboard space for diagramming, labeling, and planning research. The walls are filled with student work; as well, the walls host designated spaces for anchor charts and images to illustrate what researchers, artists, journalists, historians, map-makers, and authors, do.

While the Primary students are in these Imagination classes, the Junior students are next door, fast at work in their Innovation (STEM) class. Similarly, they move in pairs between STEM stations gaining mini-STEM lessons taught by the Math and Science specialist. These centers have attractive displays with printed words and images to advance vocabulary and directions. The inclusion of maker spaces, designated places for chess instruction, and an in-class STEM library, adds much to this Innovation class. Similarly, these rooms also have work tables with whiteboard painted surfaces, floor tiles featuring number lines, and a massive rug displaying a colorful 100's chart. Alongside the walls filled with students work are images of scientists, engineers, mathematicians, environmentalists, inventors, and researchers. In both the Imagination and Innovation classroom, computers are easily accessible at each station as a reference or research tool. Projectors are also mounted for various student and staff presentations.

By noon, it is time for lunch; students go outside to sit at picnic tables or simply eat in their classrooms. Music, ideally of the calming kind, is played to reduce any tendency to rush through eating; manners and respect are reinforced by supervising staff, interns and older student leaders. Following lunch at 12:30 p.m. the Junior students go to their Liberal Arts classroom and the Primary students head off to their STEM class. The specialist Liberal Arts teacher remains in the Imagination classroom; as well, the STEM teacher remains in the Innovation classroom space.

At 2 p.m., it is time for Fine Arts and Physical Education. Each semester features a different focus on the arts: Music, Visual Arts, or Drama. Having a gymnasium, climbing wall, and outside play area are ideal for this quality Physical Education program. By 4 p.m., school ends with a complementary check-out process where staff issue immediate kudos and a high five for a safe trip home.

In the third semester, beginning in the Junior grades, students take part in 2-hour concentrated World Languages class, emphasizing both skill in speaking a foreign language, as well as being introduced to the Social Studies of the language and its culture. Table 19.1 outlines a sample primary and junior student schedule.

At New School, homework is not assigned to the Primary and Junior students. With a 7-hour school day, there is ample time for students to practice skills and apply their understandings. And unlike the regime of some schools, sporting a culture of "quiet in the halls," New School is all about the necessary noise of excited young learners—happy to be with each other and eager to be part of an engaged learning culture. New School replaces conventional homework, with "Family Projects." Parents and students team up to co-construct different artifacts that demonstrate their learning together (a family flag; a new island, a book of billions, a new continent, a new insect, etc.). Parents have permission to be co-learners (and teachers) when they can talk with their children about researching ideas and planning for their project presentations. At the end of each semester, they co-present their projects.

Table 19.1 Sample Primary and Junior Schedule

Time	Primary Tuesday–Friday	Junior Tuesday–Friday
9:00 a.m.	Open Ceremony and Community Works Class	Open Ceremony and Community Works Class
10:00 a.m.	Recess, Fitness, and Energy Break	
10:30 a.m.	Imagination Class (Integrated Liberal Arts)	Innovation Class (Integrated STEM)
12 noon	Lunch	
12:30 p.m.	Innovation Class (Integrated STEM)	Imagination Class (Integrated Liberal Arts)
2 p.m.	Fine Arts	Physical Education
3 p.m.	Physical Education	Fine Arts
4 p.m.	Dismissal	

The costs of these volunteer teachers (parents): zero, but the benefits are far reaching.

At New School, there are no Day 1. Day 2, Day 3, Day 4, Day 5, Day 6, Day 7, or Day 8 day schedules; rather the schedule for learning is more predictable, using the natural days of the week (Monday, Tuesday, Wednesday, Thursday, and Friday) that are used by people outside the school walls.

A DAY IN THE LIFE OF A SIXTH THROUGH TENTH GRADE STUDENT AT NEW SCHOOL

In the Middle School wing of a New School, a student in sixth through tenth grade begins the day in a co-ed Community Works class. This course features character education, career building, and peer teaching preparatory units, as well as service learning and health education. Following this advisory supported class, the female students move on to their single-gender morning Liberal Arts class, followed by their STEM block classes in the afternoon. The male students begin the school day in their STEM block classes and then move to their Liberal Arts classes in the afternoon. Tables 19.2 and 19.3 illustrate the first and second semester schedules for students in sixth through eighth grade while tables 19.4 and 19.5 illustrate the first two semesters for students in ninth and tenth grade. Note these are the schedules for Tuesday to Friday classes; students work in co-ed groups on Macro Monday projects, electives and field trip experiences.

In the third semester, students continue in their single-gender groupings with their World Languages classes in a half-day concentrated program that includes instruction from master language teachers who also integrate the class with Social Studies. For the final half of the day, students have the option of working on an independent or collaborative research study, upgrading any work to a mastery level (80% understanding), with Grade 9

Table 19.2 Semester 1 New Middle Prep School Programming

Time	Middle Prep (6–8) Girls Program (Tuesday–Friday)	Middle Prep (6–8) Boys Program (Tuesday–Friday)
9:00 a.m.	Open Ceremony and Community Works class	Open Ceremony and Community Works class
10:00 a.m.	English Language Arts (fiction)	Science
12 noon	Lunch	
12:30 p.m.	Science	English Language Arts (fiction)
2:30 p.m.	Fine Arts	Physical Education
3:15 p.m.	Physical Education	Fine Arts
4 p.m.	Dismissal	

Table 19.3 Semester 2 New Middle School Programming

Time	Middle Prep (6–8) Boys Program (Tuesday–Friday)	Middle Prep (6–8) Girls Program (Tuesday–Friday)
9:00 a.m.	Open Ceremony and Community Works class	Open Ceremony and Community Works class
10:00 a.m.	Liberal Arts (Social Science, Inquiry and English Language Arts (non-fiction)	Mathematics
12 noon	Lunch	
12:30 p.m.	Mathematics	Liberal Arts (Social Science, Inquiry and English Language Arts (non-fiction)
2:30 p.m.	Fine Arts	Physical Education
3:15 p.m.	Physical Education	Fine Arts
4 p.m.	Dismissal	

Table 19.4 Semester 1 New Junior High School Programming

Time	Junior High (9–10) Girls Program (Monday–Thursday)	Junior High (9–10) Boys Program (Monday–Thursday)
9:00 a.m.	Open Ceremony and Community Works class	Open Ceremony and Community Works class
10:00 a.m.	English Language Arts (fiction)	Science
12 noon	Lunch	
12:30 p.m.	Science	English Language Arts (fiction)
2:30 p.m.	Fine Arts	Physical Education
3:15 p.m.	Physical Education	Fine Arts
4 p.m.	Dismissal	

Table 19.5 Semester 2 New Junior High Programming

Time	Junior High (9–10) Boys Program (Monday–Thursday)	Junior High (9–10) Girls Program (Monday–Thursday)
9:00 a.m.	Open Ceremony and Community Works class	Open Ceremony and Community Works class
10:00 a.m.	Liberal Arts (Social Science, Inquiry and English Language Arts (non-fiction)	Mathematics
12 noon	Lunch	
12:30 p.m.	Mathematics	Liberal Arts (Social Science, Inquiry and English Language Arts (non-fiction)
2:30 p.m.	Fine Arts	Physical Education
3:15 p.m.	Physical Education	Fine Arts
4 p.m.	Dismissal	

and 10 students having the option of taking Senior high school course work in advance.

A DAY IN THE LIFE OF A GRADES 11 AND 12 STUDENT AT NEW SCHOOL

Students in their final two years at New School can take two twelfth grade credits or AP credits at one time in four semesters over two years. Students also take one co-op course in one semester that entails upwards of two months in an internship role in a local business or service industry off campus. As well, students must complete a research course and defend and publish a study. Students also have the option of taking a concentrated course (single full day course) in the third semester or taking early entry courses at a local college.

The organization and re-chunking of courses is also an innovative feature of New School. Often the volume of content in twelfth grade credit courses is difficult for many students to master. For instance, New School breaks down some of these courses, such as Biology, into two separate courses. In the grade 9 and 10 Science class, students focus on Grade 12 anatomy, zoology, botany and ecology in one semester, and then take a different course that focuses exclusively on the Kreb cycle and genetics in another semester. Together, these courses give students their grade 12 biology credit in advance of eleventh grade. Table 19.6 illustrates the Senior schedule at New School.

NEW SCHOOL AS AN IMAGE OF GREATNESS

For this inquiry into how much a great school cost, we defined greatness as "inspired learning through responsible actions within an inclusive culture."

Table 19.6 New Senior High Programming (Semesters 1 and 2)

Time	Senior High (Grades 11–12) Co-ed Program (Monday–Thursday)
9:00 a.m.	Open Ceremony and Community Works class
10:00 a.m.	Credit Course 1
12 noon	Lunch
12:30 p.m.	Credit Course 2
2:30 p.m.	Research/Activity Time
4 p.m.	Dismissal/After School Programming

All schools aim to be great. A serious commitment to innovation and school reform can help schools move beyond their current history.

Inspired Learning

Inspired learning in this New School focuses on many innovative conditions within six emerging categories that reveal how the New School can be distinct from existing conventional schools. I would argue that such conditions lay the groundwork for inspired learning and teaching, relative to Staff development and supervision; instruction and class size; curriculum and programming; and staffing and leadership; facilities and resources; vision and school size.

Staff Development and Supervision
Innovations in a New School

- regular professional development built in once a month for reflection, planning and generating innovative curriculum materials
- fair, consistent, thorough, and collaborative performance reviews; staff members self-assess their work according to benchmarks of comprehensive best practices
- staff members create portfolios that highlight their professional actions on a yearly basis—with dedicated time afforded to work on them
- more balanced breaks (sleeping in on monthly "Happy Fridays"; week-long breaks in the Fall, Winter, and at the end of March)
- mentor teachers take part in co-planning and co-teaching with mentees on a weekly basis, and work deliberately at making progress in targeted areas for improvement; mentor teachers provide feedback based on one formative observation
- parents, teachers, and community members participate in collaborative learning activities about best practices and current research in education (i.e., "Chalk Talks" that emulate more interactive Ted Talks)
- school is a member of professional associations to keep up with current research and new ideas for best practice
- input gathered when school takes part in rigorous accreditation process (i.e., Middle States Accreditation; Advanced Education, CAIS, IB, etc.)

Instruction and Class Size Innovations in a New School

- purposely small in class-size (10–16 students in a class is ideal to maximize learning and form lasting relationships with reduction in disciplines issues)

- reduced teacher: student ratio enables more individualized instruction, support, and tracking of mastery
- teachers work with same students over several years (looping) to provide ongoing enrichment or remediation, as needed
- students can work at own pace (move beyond grade level expectations or consolidate understandings when/if remediation is necessary)
- no artificial age barriers in multi-grade classrooms—moves away from a "once size fits all" pacing guide
- longer classes (60–90 minutes) enable teachers to identify and provide immediate support for students who may have misunderstandings
- single-gender classrooms in grades 6 through 10 allow for tailoring learning to ideal gender learning conditions
- older students support younger students in multi-grade and peer teaching settings
- students organized strategically in pairs to increase talk and enhance appreciation for all voices
- collaborative culture and sense of belonging is central to reducing loneliness and unhappiness

Curriculum and Programming Innovations in a New School

- time to apply understandings and delve deeper in topics in 90-minute classes
- engage in a natural routine whereby the same classes are taught at the same time Monday through Thursday
- daily Physical Education and Fine Arts in younger grades stimulate overall intellectual capacity
- increased time for Science and application of scientific practice
- local community utilized as important contexts for learning
- all students participate in intramurals clubs, arts groups, or athletic teams and report card includes this involvement in co-curricular programming
- students given more chances and help to meet expectations; rare to leave much learning behind—re-testing and upgrading is a natural part of the culture
- view standardized test scores as one part of the assessment pie
- reduction in number of kids "falling through the cracks"
- creativity and inquiry are cornerstones of the curriculum

Students also know how to conduct research and inquiry, not only making sense of things, but for designing new things, ideally things that have not been invented yet. Making something that wasn't there, or quite there before, can be inspiring. Creativity, in this sense is not about completing a recipe for making a rocket and then launching it. For creativity to be of a higher order, students are involved in designing rockets, beyond the assemblage of directions. Creativity, at the New School, is a priority; community members are not obsessed with gathering lower-level facts on standardized tests.

In an OECD working paper, Lucas, Claxton and Spencer (2013) claimed that the "lack of any requirement to assess creativity in a national, summative way (or even formatively in class) also contributes to the undervaluing of creativity" (p. 9). They added: "But the lack of school-friendly tools to assess creativity is arguably another reason for paying less attention to creativity" (p. 9). At New School, innovative tools for assessing creativity are being developed, piloted, and revised based on ongoing input from students and staff.

Leadership and Staffing Innovations in a New School

- teachers co-teach with teacher-leaders who also teach classes part-time
- staff members take on leadership roles, so talent pool is rich with experience and potential (a culture "crawling with leaders")
- teacher-leaders selected to present at various conferences, such as ASCD, NCTE, NCTM, and NSTA

Resources and Facilities Innovations in a New School

- inspiring learning spaces, like Disney detailing each part of an attraction
- school grounds, entranceway, halls, and classrooms highlight distinctness of school
- students surrounded by inspiring posters and student work honoring evidence of ongoing learning (not staring at blank walls or perfectly staged condos)

Vision and School Size Innovations in a New School

- Small school (< 300 students in K-8 school or < 600 students K-12)
- school meets or exceeds standards, and provides ample evidence of student learning
- commitment to co-learning is evident in parent and teacher workshops and family projects
- students work collaboratively with community members to solve local problems
- aims to be a model school with university affiliations, not for replicating, but for inspiring a generation of new laboratory schools
- cohesive vertical alignment for disciplines in K-12 school

- multi-grade classrooms allow the same teacher over several years, to not let understandings of less than 80% be left behind

RESPONSIBLE ACTIONS

To imagine a New School is one thing, but to afford it requires responsible actions taken by key decision-makers, fiercely focused on creating ideal conditions for all students to succeed. Student success is often addressed over the long term using quantitative metrics such as graduation rates, college acceptances, college graduation rates, scholarships/bursaries, and in some cases, future salaries. Data in the short-term tends to focus on standardized test scores and school attendance. The assumption is that investing in actions that generate such data points is the only significant way to provide evidence of student success.

A school, however, is much more complex, than a simple input-output model. Educational decision-makers, who support more complex learning experiences than teaching for a test, are indeed demonstrating responsible actions. When both quantitative and qualitative gains are valued, schools can plan for success in the short and long term.

Building great schools does not mean we need more money or need to tax existing scarce resources. We simply need to use funds differently. At New School, for instance, students graduate having a plethora of experiences and knowing how to do many things including how to: play chess, bridge, cribbage; make a website; make a robot; write and publish a novel or non-fiction text; change a tire; drive things with engines (cars, boats, ATV's, snowmobiles, etc.); make a vehicle; build a shed/house/outdoor theater; prepare a budget; write a check; submit an invention for a patent; volunteer at a senior's home; at a hospital; local pet shelter, etc.; play the piano and another instrument; demonstrate multiple genres of dance; and, run a mile in under 10 minutes, and swim 50 lengths. And whether students make a positive difference in other people's lives matters, too. Such a qualitative list of outcomes is part of this New School curriculum for all students; such experiences should not be optional.

INCLUSIVE CULTURE

The emphasis on an inclusive culture is often left out of the core values mix of conventional schools that tend to focus so much on individualism. At this New School, cooperation and collaboration are considered central features of a great school. The Community Works class is embedded within the curriculum to bring attention to the wealth of self-less acts of generosity that support learning about character, service learning, and health education. New School builds inclusive cultures so that all students and staff feel like they belong. Rather than address mental health issues in a reactive way, a focus on building a positive school climate is a proactive commitment to teaching the whole child and appreciating the whole adult in the learning community.

At New School, we plan for fun and we plan for happiness. All staff members see personal and social learning as part of their teaching role; as well, they receive ongoing counseling training, not as experts, but as frontline first aiders—people willing to lend a hand, whenever the need arises. Given that animals can have the power of releasing endorphins, New School will feature comfort dogs, goats, and aquariums full of fish, to add to caring acts for as many green plants as possible!

It's hard to have an inclusive school when everyone does not know everyone else's name. According to the OECD (2012), "schools may benefit from alternative organisation of learning time, including . . . the size of schools" (p. 4). They add: "In some cases, creating smaller classrooms and schools can be a policy to reinforce student-student and student-teacher interactions and better learning strategies" (pp. 11–12). New School is purposely small in numbers and class size. At this school, discipline is not the subject of much attention, as there are fewer unhappy community members. Educators teach and learn as collaborators, not "champions" of a teacher-directed classroom.

This New School is not about conformity. The inclusive culture provides opportunities for all community members to have a say in what happens at the school. In traditional school settings, students rarely have much input into what they will learn or how they will learn. At this New School, students in each grade have opportunities to weigh in on the inclusiveness (or not) of the culture. Primary students draw and label images of how they feel included at school, while Junior-aged students, and above, fill out detailed surveys. Such data is reviewed on an annual basis to test the integrity of the assertion that this school has an inclusive culture for all students. Staff members and families take part in these surveys, as well, so that all stakeholders have a voice in school matters.

At New School, the culture is driven by reform and innovation—polar "opposites" of conformity. The vibrancy and mental health of all community members matter. The quality character program is proactive, allowing students to reflect on their learning, their choices, and how they relate to each other. Teachers at New School understand the difference between conformity and engagement. Furthermore, they feel empowered to build their own curriculum and are not force-fed by "paint-by-numbers" formulas developed by others outside their classrooms.

Just as a subject can be more connected to other subjects, so too, should schools form solid links to the community. At New School the playgrounds were co-planned with many community members. Inside the school, students and staff weighed in; outside the school, the local parks and recreation department, police, and neighbors also had say. By sharing the design, construction and maintenance of a playground, the community uses it at other times when school is not in operation. The risk is shared with the community, so locks, fencing and 24-hour surveillance are reduced shared costs.

To understand and develop an inclusive culture, New School community members are open and welcoming of other cultures. Students have many opportunities to learn World Languages that are a window into global cultures. This New School blends second language (or more) acquisition within a Social Studies context. Language is a key component of culture, not separate from it. Building courses that teach about a language and the country of origin, as well as their reach around the world, provides a meaningful context for learning. By comparing local and global cultures, and different languages, New School comes to understand the commonalities and distinctions among humanity, and by understanding others, we aim to be more inclusive.

So many silos between disciplines have separated second language acquisition from the study of history, geography, and economics. What is at the heart of a nation—is their language. Furthermore, the study of languages that are spoken outside the homeland are also sources of an enriching learning experience. Rather than have a 40-minute daily Spanish or French class, this New School increased time for the World Language class by focusing close to a half day of study each day in the third semester. In this way, learning a new language does not compete with six or seven other subjects at the same time.

A New School was imagined as a synthesis of research, insight, and experience. A school looking to improve practice, beyond the traditional model, can view this New School model as a collection of options that have the potential to move the school success needle in more positive directions. We can do much more than host elaborate pep rallies before standardized test week, or give out bigger trophies for perfect attendance. We can embrace systematic change and we can afford it.

Grappling with Ideas

- What would be your ideal school schedule? Share your ideas with a classmate.
- Make a list of reforms that you would like to see happen in your school.

Part 5

THE CURRENCY OF CHANGE

If people were silent nothing would change.

—Malala Yousafzai

THE CURRENCY OF CHANGE

In this final section and chapter, we compare the possibilities to respond to this question: To change or not to change? It can be difficult for new schools to take shape without stakeholders being aware of more options for schooling than what currently exists. Learning about what else in education is happening around the world and teasing out if the ideas capture interest is a missed step in school improvement. Furthermore, making determinations if we can afford something else is also remiss in strategic plans. It's time as Malala suggests to speak up and reset the education compass toward new directions.

Chapter 20

To Change or Not to Change ... That Is the Question ...

The New School presented one way of synthesizing a series of great practices in education. Understanding how much a great school can cost, can help move the needle on whether or not schools, ready for reform will take steps toward change, or not. This final chapter adds a hypothetical comparison of costs associated with the New School and the ways traditional schools tend to spend their funds.

HOW MUCH DOES A GREAT SCHOOL COST COMPARED TO A CONVENTIONAL SCHOOL?

For the most part, by re-purposing how funds are spent, and by building in ample time to design and implement change, it is possible to improve at the same time as afford quality schools for ALL students. Comparing the costs of New School, relative to a sample conventional school, involved reviewing various funding, staffing, and leasing documents. Even though less money can be generated from student funding for New School, as classrooms are capped at a 20:1 teacher: student ratio, the differences in expenses between the two models did not reveal that there were significant savings overall in the larger school or classroom size model with a higher teacher: student ratio (25:1).

Table 20.1 illustrates how a sample income statement from this New School, housing 160 students and 14 staff members, might compare with a sample K-12 conventional school, housing 900 students and 63 staff members.

Within each expenditure category lies specific opportunities for change. Tracking the cost of building and sustaining a great school is no easy task,

Table 20.1 Comparison of Pro Forma Income Statements for New School and Sample Conventional School

Budget Items and Notes	New School	Conventional School
Revenue: $15,000/student	$2,400,000.00 (160 students)	$13,500,000.00 (900 students)
Teacher:student ratio (regular classrooms)	20:1	25:1
Staffing costs		
• Teaching staff (including benefits)	$540,000.00 (~23%) 9 teaching staff	$3,060,000.00 (23%) 51 teaching staff
• Non-teaching staff (including benefits)	$120,000.00 (~5%) 3 non-teaching staff	$400,000.00 (~3%) 10 non-teaching staff
• School leaders (including benefits)	$145,000.00 (~6%) (1 principal + 3 part-time VP's—$15,000 stipend each)	$500,000.00 (~4%) (2 P + 2 AP's)
• Staff development	$120,000.00 (~5%)	$675,000.00 (~5%)
Out-sourced services/products		
• Insurance	$22,880.00 (~1%)	$128,700.00 (<1%)
• Legal fees	$20,000.00 (<1%)	$112,500.00 (<1%)
• Auditors and accounting	$20,000.00 (<1%)	$95,000.00 (<1%)
• Cleaning and custodial services	$52,800.00 (~2%)	$316,800.00 (~2%)
Direct student impact expenditures		
• Academic and co-curricular materials	$400,000.00 (~17%)	$2,295,000.00 (~17%)
• Technology (hardware)	$200,000.00 (~8%)	$1,020,000.00 (~8%)
• Transportation (field trips)	$200,000.00 (~8%)	$1,020,000.00 (~8%)
• Food services	0	$840,000.00 (~6%)
Facility, utilities, and security expenditures		
• Facility rent/mortgage paymnts	$231,680.00 (~10%)	$1,303,200.00 (~10%)
• Utilities: heating/electricity/water	$39,600.00 (~2%)	$223,200.00 (~2%)
• Maintenance	$56,320.00 (~2%)	$294,300.00 (~2%)
Administrative costs		
• Communications/staff computers	$75,000.00 (~3%)	$420,000.00 (~3%)
• Printing/office materials	$75,000.00 (~3%)	$420,000.00 (~3%)
Overall expenses	$2,318,280.00	$13,123,700.00
Balance	$81,720.00	$376,300.00

but by viewing school financial statements, it is possible to make room for substantial innovation.

The percentage proportions were included to show how the funding pie can be distributed. As well, these data sources will become dated, but the weighting of different expenditure groupings might prove to be helpful guidelines.

Values are reflected in the ways funds are spent and the way funds are generated. In this simplistic comparison, it was assumed that students in both New School and this sample conventional school would be funded at a rate of $15,000 per student. While this figure represents a lower tuition fee than the ask of many independent and private schools, it does match more with higher publicly funded schools. Unfortunately, there are states that allocate less funds for their public schools.

Calculations for each school clearly show that there is more revenue for schools with more students and classrooms with fewer students in them. Nevertheless, if it is possible to reduce spending, there would be less need for additional revenue. There are also alternative ways of generating funds and sharing costs (as outlined in chapter 18). Schools that provide time for staff to apply for grants and seek donations recognize that some new initiatives may require additional funding.

It is possible to reduce classroom and school sizes by re-purposing how money is spent in schools.

Shifting Staffing Costs

Like most educational institutions, staffing represents the largest expenditure category. The percentage of school expenditures afforded to salaries and benefits for the conventional school sample is roughly 35%, whereas New School's staffing is higher at 39%. For an additional 4%, students and teachers benefit from smaller class sizes. If you did a mockup of figures with 25 students in each of New School class, the overall revenue would increase to $3,000,0000, with the staffing expenditures at the New School coming in well below the conventional school sample of 35%.

The average teacher salary in the conventional example and New School estimate that both schools pay staff well (average $60,000). What the staff is responsible for at this New School, however, is distinct from the sample conventional school. Teachers in the New School are specialists in either STEM or Liberal Arts; unlike many elementary schools, there is an equal distribution of these talents. Teachers who teach Math must also be qualified to teach Science; and teachers who teach ELA, must also be qualified to teach Social Studies.

At New School the layers of administrative bureaucracy are flattened, reducing the gap between the school leader and the teachers and students on the ground level. In a typical high school, the principal may have two or three vice principals, mainly responsible for behavior oversight, with upwards of a dozen department heads, responsible for development and supervision of their subject-specific teaching teams. In the elementary, primary, junior, and middle school, "division heads" often take on mentorship and supervisory type roles.

Quality control is at risk when leaders or supervisors are stretched too thin. "Superschools," using conventional organizational charts, illustrate a diseconomy of scale, as the need for more staff means that more administrators would be needed to supervise them, and more support staff to support more administrators. With embedded teaching responsibilities, school leaders have a direct line of sight, not only of staff, but a direct pulse on students as teaching is part of what they do. Given the costs of human capital and the increased costs of administrative salaries, keeping the school small is do-able with a keen eye to shifting responsibilities. A school should be as large as the quality of supervision and support can manage.

New School would require nine teachers (three of which are part-time administrators) with one school leader. The sample conventional school would need fifty-one teachers with four full-time administrators: a principal for the high school and a separate principal for the elementary part of the school with one assistant principal for each. The school leader salaries ranged from $100,000 in New School to an average of $125,000 for the principals and vice principals in the conventional K-12 school example. In New School, each part-time administrator received $75,000, an increase of $15,000 above their teaching salary.

This New School increases the number of part-time administrators at the same time as reducing the overall staffing needs; all administrators, including the school leader, teach. Having multiple part-time administrative roles builds in many teacher–leader development opportunities at New School. Figure 20.1 illustrates New School organizational chart.

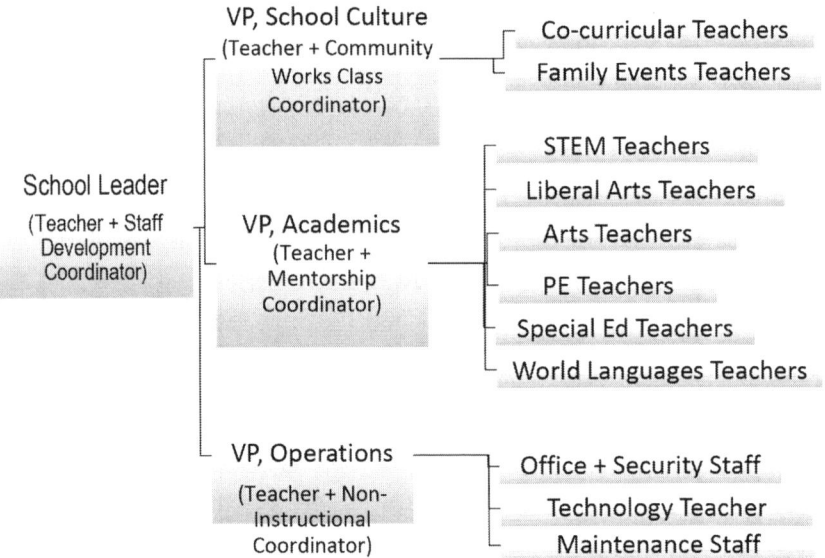

Figure 20.1 New School Organizational Chart.

Investing in staff is not an option at New School; $120,000 would be set aside for fourteen staff members. It is doubtful, however, that conventional schools with 900 students allocate $675,000 for the development of 63 staff members. A more realistic conventional school budget for staff development tends to be less than 2%, an estimated value less than $300,000. By investing in staff, there are also savings in reducing turnover, and the need to continuously search for talent that ultimately will need development on site anyway.

In this New School, the teachers teach four days a week adding significant time for rest/planning with the same comparative salary. At the New School, staff are provided with PD funding for local workshops, and every attempt is made to fully fund staff who are selected to present at conferences outside the community. Specifically, this school is a member of many professional associations including ASCD (Association for Supervision Curriculum and Development), NCTE (National Council for Teachers of English), NCTM (National Council for Teachers of Mathematics), and NSTA (National Science Teachers Association).

While economists have not punched the exact numbers about the short- and long-term savings from professional development and quality supervision, there is no doubt that such an investment and recognition of cost benefits is long overdue. Even though 5% of the operational expenses were allocated for staff development for both New School and the conventional school model, this is not representative of most school budgets.

Revising Student-Directed Expenditures

While a higher percentage of expenses are required to hire more teachers for lower class sizes in New School, there are significant ways New School saves on student-directed spending. Rather than allocating robust funds for textbooks and teacher guides, New School focuses on the development of less expensive customized academic materials, field trips, and technology. For instance, significant funding is allocated for each grade grouping for robotics, which means all students are guaranteed robotics instruction. In a conventional school, however, robotics instruction tends to exist for only a few students after school.

In some jurisdictions, regular testing programs for conventional schools can cost upwards of $25,000. At New School, standardized tests are only administered at the beginning of Grades 3, 6, and 11 to compare mastery from classroom assessments with the standardized score results, for purposes of adjusting curriculum. At the district or state level, there are more cost savings associated with reducing the number of annual grade tests, and the number of staff needed to manage the tests, that questionably declare which schools are better than others, based on such scores.

Where New School deviates sharply from the norm is how it funds for transportation and meals. How funds are used for transportation are significantly different between a conventional school and New School. There are considerable funds saved by not providing door-to-door pick-up and delivery service, five days a week. In a New School model, there are more (smaller) schools in walking distance of the school. In some cases, students also have easy access to public transportation.

Busing, however, for students from rural income and less dense areas would be provided. In most communities, however, there would be no need for allocating funds for regular busing, bus drivers, maintenance of busses, and bus monitors in areas where students could walk to school. Funds for transporting students for volunteer experiences, internships, or research on a weekly basis, however, are budgeted for, so that students can be a part of authentic learning situations inside their local communities. It is rare for conventional schools to fund regular field trips.

At New School, students are required to bring their own lunches. In many conventional schools, the education budget provides free meals for students who qualify for free and reduced lunches and breakfasts. At New School, the costs for such meals are covered by state or provincial health and welfare budgets. Families who require breakfast, lunch, and dinner support are provided for by one governmental agency responsible for directly helping families in need. All students need nourishment to learn. Food Services have traditionally been absorbed by education budgets; re-thinking such costs is worthy of further discussion. By not budgeting for food and cafeteria staff, this New School uses these savings to fund other often depleted educational areas of the budget.

Updating Facility, Utilities, and Security Expenditures

Abramson's *School Construction Repor*t (2015) was referenced to average the elementary, middle and high school square footage recommendations for each student to project facility costs for a sample "conventional" school of 900 students, and New School with 160 students. Initially, the scale was designated for an average elementary school of 625 students, a middle school of 610 students, and a high school averaging 1,000 students. The average of all three schools (181 square feet per student), was then multiplied by the estimated cost per square foot ($212/square foot) to build a new school.

Using Abramson's estimates: the sample "conventional school" would cost approximately $35,534,800 to build from scratch, while New School would cost $6,139,520. With depreciation over 25 years, the costs to carry these facilities would be approximately $1,381,392 and $245,580 annually. U.S. rates for renting office space, warehouse space, and industrial space, and examined the range of costs in cities where the cost per square foot was much higher than other locations were examined. The leased estimate cost of $8/per square foot for each school (New School: $231,680/year; sample Conventional School: $1,303,200/year) in each financial statement, turned out to be about 10% of the total operating costs, less than the 13% listed as the national average costs for U.S. Charter Schools (National Alliance Public Charter Schools, 2013, p. 1). While these numbers are not representative by any means, given the small sample size of schools, they do function to compare two draft sketches of facility costs that compare a New School with a conventional school budget.

It is anticipated that much more school funding will be needed to address rising safety and security issues. More funds will be required to manage new security features in schools, and as schools adapt, they will need to increase the maintenance portions of their budgets.

SO HOW MUCH DOES A GREAT SCHOOL COST?

What are the costs of reform? Few studies exist about financing school reform, yet many accounts of failed reform fill the pages of documents and autopsies of ideas gone south. Start-up funds, grants, and many short-term incentives have been spent in the search for *Holy Grail* answers in education.

What makes it difficult to carry out innovative designs of new schools is the tendency to gravitate toward a "sameness," propelled by conventional ways public schools allot their funds. While the elegance of replicating a perfectly executed budget may be entrancing for some, it is still possible to be adrift without a rudder of school values driving the numbers.

The costs associated with any school depends on whether one is being transformed or built from scratch. Simple changes in demographics can change the nature of a school, creating a need to enlarge it, or accommodate for fewer students. The budget is often referred to as the point at which the "rubber meets the road." In the case of New School, it is where great ideas meet the bottom line and pass the test of affordability. Schools may list lofty goals that support ambitious visions, but it is the economic reality that defines the degree to which a school will do what it says it will do, well. The school budget is a mirror of what the members of the school community not only value, but can afford.

Planning for reform is about designing better options for teaching and learning, and finding more ways to use funds and to generate funds when needed to "move the cheese" of conventional schooling. A great school does much more than make ends meet.

Rather than what innovations can fit into an existing school budget, how is it that school budgets can be flexible enough to respond more to student needs?

Once stakeholders are more aware of possibilities for change, they can determine whether the costs involved, not only in terms of funding, but the time to plan and implement and monitor new initiatives, are worth the investment.

Defining what schools value is at the heart of ensuring that the school mission, vision, and goals are in alignment with the school budget. The building of new schools can synthesize ideal practices that can be affordable. Rather than beginning with an end in mind, it can be more about beginning with values in mind, and letting those values shape a more inspiring education story.

Stakeholders who step off-road and take a deep dive look at the possibilities for best practices, can deepen their values, understandings and horizons. When we can understand a big picture of education, we can build meaningful rudders to steer our way in more constructive schooling directions.

And how do new schools avoid replicating the values of existing schools? It may come down to how new schools define greatness. Some individuals may view greatness as high test scores, perfect attendance and all things quantifiable, while others aim to be much more.

The intent of crafting an imaginary New School was to share an example of moving beyond "good enough" targets. Unfortunately, many decision-makers tend to follow predictable funding formulas that frame more conventional models of schooling. As well, funding agencies, impressed by data dashboard metrics, often view greatness through the same limited data lens. When decision-makers narrow their view of what constitutes greatness, it can be difficult for schools to implement significant change.

Being aware of outlier ideas and ways to make change affordable goes hand in hand. Solutions do not have to be dependent upon new cash added to the fire; change can come about through the redistribution of existing funds. The school budget is a barometer. By generating dialogue about what ideal schools can be, we can backward design from these value sets, what it would cost to build and sustain them. Look at school budgets through Biden's lens and think about what you see:

> Don't tell me what you value, show me your budget, and I'll tell you what you value.—Joe Biden

Epilogue

How will people respond to this view of school economies and values? I asked Rick Wormeli, educational writer, leader, and author of the best-selling book Fair Isn't Always Equal, *to respond to these ideas. I believe Rick's message is worthy of reflection as we fast forward into what could be future budget and value considerations.*

FAST FORWARD BY RICK WORMELI

Re-aligning financial priorities with personal values in order to make substantive progress instead of simply shrugging off budget constraints and program disappointments with a *There's-nothing-we-can-do-it's-the-way-it's-always-been-done* is pure oxygen. Breathe it deeply, and feel the rejuvenation that comes with it, as you read Barbara J. Smith's wonderful book *How Much Does a Great School Cost? Insights on School Economies and School Values*.

One of the biggest stressors in our education field is to work in misalignment with one's values. In such situations, we are on edge, negotiating with ourselves daily for how far we are willing to stray from our authentic person.

A second stressor, particularly in education, is the lack of funding and resources to act upon what we perceive is needed for basic instruction, let alone true effectiveness, especially with an increasingly diverse student body and politically motivated, but pedagogically corrupt accountability measures.

We don't have to educate like this.

In *How Much Does a Great School Cost*, Smith shreds our hypocrisies and replaces them with true hope and real practicality. While reading, our political spines are stiffened and creativity soars. This is the work of a consummate professional, a clear-eyed and compassionate educator that gets things done with steadfast integrity. From a lifetime of dedicated service to generations of students and teachers in North America, Smith's thinking here provides the research and behind-the-scenes instructional awareness, prioritizing, negotiations, and creative budget balancing needed to live up to the promise of inspired, equitable, and highly effective education in the modern era.

This content is candid, however, she does not condescend to the reader; it's not for the faint-hearted. She asks educators to know their stuff and accept their influential roles in student achievement.

In both my formal training and professional experience, I've read endless texts on school leadership, instructional design, managing the physical and human capital of schools, and more, but I'm gobsmacked by Smith's work here.

This is stewardship in its finest form. And get this, Smith shows real solutions for funding programs and materials, not just in what are commonly considered "core" subjects, but also in physical education, fine and performing arts, students' personal maturation/tenacity, social-emotional learning, teacher creativity, technology, professional development, food services, civic education, internships, service learning experiences, critical thinking, performance reviews, libraries, differentiation, community building, intersession/afterschool programs, and particularly impactful to student success, assessment and grading reform.

In each, she walks us through the step-by-step thinking, leadership, and financing to turn stagnated aspirations actionable.

There is such cogency here. School leaders will savor the clarity and imaginative solutions to very real frustrations, and classroom practitioners will get new and divergent ideas for classroom innovation, creative funding sources, where to get materials, arranging learning spaces, and professional development. Sure, some of the suggestions are beyond a classroom teacher's control, but most of them ignite self-efficacy, no matter the role in the building.

So many times in schools we take the politically expedient path instead of the mature climb. The path of least resistance wins, and students can't help but be diminished in our race toward complacency. It's ossifying. Climbing always reveals more, however, it strengthens our conviction and gets oxygen to the brain. From such perspectives, we see the farthest and choose the most efficient course. With such provisioning, classroom instruction is revitalized, students learn well.

In a particularly exciting chapter near the end of the book, Smith describes what life would be like for teachers and students in an imaginary school if it were governed by the education values and financial acumen described in this book. If you read it first to see where's she's heading, you might think it's impossible, the stuff of fantasy. A secret part of you, however, will marvel. You'll find it strangely similar to your original reasons for becoming an educator. *Wow,* you think as you read from the book from its beginning, *she's provided example after example of is really happening in school after school. There's solid research and application here,* you continue, *We can actually do this.*

This book gives poorly resourced, uncreative, overcrowded, or underdeveloped schools, and those faculties who are financially inconsistent with their stated values, a running start at greatness. The policies here create the school in which I would want to teach, and even more telling, the school where I would want to educate my own children.

Living our values makes teaching real, and positive things get done. Many days, however, it feels like we're pale shadows pretending to do school, that we've settled for the mere semblance of instruction, but not real instruction that's meaningful, lasts, or reflects our stated mission. It feels justified, however, because most of our What-if?'s over the years are confronted immediately with cries of no money, and in some cases, divisive politics. We're told to stretch the few resources we have even further and make do, to avoid innovation that might pose uncomfortable change. A steady diet of shackled pedagogy, dashed hopes, and cynicism can lead good people to half-hearted efforts in the classroom—or to other professions entirely.

So, let's stop pretending, let's dream big. Let's really "do school" effectively, turning it into something great. Given Smith's innovative and professional suggestions in these pages, it's clear we have the budget to act upon our values; it's time to connect the two. Rarely has creative school budgeting expressed such integrity, rarely has it been so professionally invigorating.

Rick Wormeli
Education Writer/Leader
Author, *Fair Isn't Always Equal: Second Edition*
January 2019

Appendix A

U.S. Grant Opportunities

GENERAL

Fund for Teachers, http://www.fundforteachers.org

IBMImpactGrants, https://www.ibm.com/ibm/responsibility/downloads/initiatives/2016_Impact_Grants_Program_Offering_Brochure.pdf

Bill and Melinda Gates Foundation, https://www.gatesfoundation.org/How-We-Work/General-Informataion/Grant-Opportunities

Carnegie Foundation for the Advancement of Teaching, https://www.carnegiefoundation.org

Carnegie Corporation of New York, https://www.carnegie.org/grants/

Charles LaFitte Foundation, https://charleslafitte.org/grants/

Bridgestone Firestone Trust Fund, https://www.cdpublications.com/fam/o-no-deadline-bridgestonefirestone-trust-fund-offers-education-grants-2163

Deutsche Bank America Grant, https://www.db.com/usa/content/en/Grant-Guidelines.html

McCarthey Dressman Education Foundation, https://mccartheydressman.org/teacher-development-grants/

https://mccartheydressman.org/academic-enrichment-grants/

https://mccartheydressman.org/teacher-development-grants/

https://mccartheydressman.org/student-teaching-scholarshipsmentoring/

https://www.donorschoose.org

Free Career Advice from CareerVillage.org!, http://www.digitalwish.com/dw/digitalwish/grants?id=257

The Big Deal eBook Newsletters, https://www.bigdealbook.com/topics/?show=funding_recognition

Discover Collaboration Grants, http://www.discovere.org/about-us/outreach-grants/collaboration-grants

Target Field Trip Education Grants, https://corporate.target.com/corporate-responsibility/community/philanthropy

https://kidsinneedfoundation.submittable.com/submit
AIAA Foundation Classroom Grant Program,
https://www.aiaa.org/Secondary.aspx?id=4184&terms=grants
Sol Hirsch Education Fund Grants,
https://nwafoundation.org/scholarships-grants/sol-hirsch-education-fund-grants/
Grant Wrangler, http://www.grantwrangler.com/
International Paper Environmental & Literacy Education Grants, http://www.internationalpaper.com/company/regions/north-america/ip-foundation-usa/apply-for-a-grant
GrantWatch.com, https://www.grantwatch.com/all-grants.php
International Paper Environmental & Literacy Education Grants, http://www.internationalpaper.com/company/regions/north-america/ip-foundation-usa/apply-for-a-grant
NEA Foundation Student Achievement Grants, https://www.neafoundation.org/for-educators/student-achievement-grants/
NEA—Learning and Leadership Grants, https://www.neafoundation.org/for-educators/learning-and-leadership-grants/
Best Buy Community Grants, https://corporate.bestbuy.com/community-grants-page/
Sherwood Foundation Education Grants (Omaha NE), https://sherwoodfoundation.org/apply/
Freeman-McMoran Education Mini Grants, http://www.freeportinmycommunity.com/schools/mini-grants
Siouxland Communitdy Foundation Teacher Grants (Siouxland Tri-State Area), http://www.siouxlandcommunityfoundation.org/Education.aspx

LITERACY/ELA

The Laura Bush Foundation for America's Libraries, http://www.laurabushfoundation.com
ILA Regie Routman Teacher Recognition Grant, http://www.regieroutman.org/professional-development/teacher-recognition-grant/
Dollar General Literacy Foundation Grants and Programs, https://www.dgliteracy.org/grant-programs/
Barnes and Noble Community Business Development Program,
http://www.barnesandnobleinc.com/about-bn/sponsorships-charitable-donations/
Beyond Words, http://www.ala.org/aasl/awards/beyond-words
USA TODAY Electronic Edition Grants, http://usatodayeducation.com/k12/usa-today-education-grant-request
Penguin Random House Foundation Library Awards for Innovation
http://foundation.penguinrandomhouse.com/libraryawards/guidelines-and-application/

ARTS

Teens' Artistic and Cultural Advancement Program, http://www.surdna.org/what-we-fund/thriving-cultures/teens-artistic-and-cultural-advancement.html
Music Instrument Grants

STEM

Lowe's Toolbox for Education Grant, http://toolboxforeducation.com
Cisco Grants, https://www.cisco.com/c/en/us/solutions/industries/education/us-education/resources/grants-strategy.html
K-12 HP—Technology for Teaching Grant, Hewlerd Packard education grant
GE Additive Education Program, https://www.ge.com/additive/press-releases/ge-additive-education-program-accepting-applications-schools-3d-printers
Form Labs—3d printing grant, https://formlabs.com/research-3d-printing-grant/
Rockwell Collins FIRST Science and Technology Grants for Iowa Schools
Teacher Grants, $1000 for Classroom Technology
Computer Science Teacher Grants $1,000
Cyber Security Grant, http://www.digitalwish.com/dw/digitalwish/grants?id=262
Freeport-McMoran Foundation's STEM Innovation Grants, http://www.freeportinmycommunity.com/schools/stem-grant
Math Education Trust Grants, https://www.nctm.org/funding/
Verizon Innovative Learning Schools Grants, https://www.verizon.com/about/responsibility/verizon-innovative-learning
Toshiba America Foundation, http://www.toshiba.com/taf/612.jsp
MIT Grants, http://lemelson.mit.edu/inventeams
Monsanto Fund Grow Rural Education grant. https://www.americasfarmers.com/grow-rural-education/program-rules/
Beacon Technology Teacher Grant, https://fios.verizon.com/beacon/technology-teacher-grant/
National Council of Teachers of Mathematics—Emerging Teacher-Leaders in Elementary School Mathematics Grants, https://www.nctm.org/Grants-and-Awards/Grants/Emerging-Teacher-Leaders-in-Elementary-School-Mathematics-Grants/
Pets in the Classroom Grant Program, https://www.petsintheclassroom.org
National Science Teachers Association, http://www.nsta.org/about/awards.aspx
Angela Award
Distinguished Informal Science Education Awards
Distinguished Service to Science Education Awards
Distinguished Teaching Awards
DuPont Pioneer Excellence in Agricultural Science Education Award
Faraday Science Communicator Award
Maitland P. Simmons

Memorial Award for New Teachers
Ron Mardigian Memorial Bio-Rad Explorer Award
Northrop Grumman Foundation Excellence in Engineering Education Award NSTA Fellow Award
NSTA Legacy Award
Robert E. Yager Exemplary Teaching Award
Robert H. Carleton Award
SeaWorld Parks and Entertainment Outstanding Environmental Educator of the Year
Shell Science Teaching Award
Shell Urban Science Educators Development Award
Sylvia Shugrue Award for Elementary School Teachers
Vernier Technology Awards
Wendell G. Mohling Outstanding Aerospace Educator Award
Siemens STEM Day Sweepstakes, https://www.siemensstemday.com/sweepstakes
Albert Einstein Distinguished Educator Fellowship Program, https://science.energy.gov/wdts/einstein/ https://science.energy.gov/wdts/einstein/
ACS-Hach High School Chemistry Classroom Grant, https://www.acs.org/content/acs/en/funding-and-awards/grants/hachhighschool.html
Math Education Trust Grants, https://www.nctm.org/funding/
Rockwell Collins FIRST Science and Technology Grants for Iowa Schools, https://www.rockwellcollins.com/Our_Company/Corporate_Responsibility/Community_Overview/FIRST/FIRST_Grants.aspx
Toshiba Grants for Science and Mathematics, http://www.toshiba.com/taf/about.jsp
Carnagie Corporation of New York K-12 Grants for Education, https://www.insidephilanthropy.com/grants-for-k-12-education/carnegie-corporation-of-new-york-grants-for-k-12-education.html
Freeman-McMoran Education Mini Grants, http://www.freeportinmycommunity.com/schools/mini-grants
Schools, ST_Grants.aspx
American Honda Foundation Grants, https://www.honda.com/community/applying-for-a-grant
Presidential Awards for Excellence in Science and Math Teaching, https://www.paemst.org

SOCIAL STUDIES/COMMUNITY/ CHARACTER EDUCATION GRANTS

$3000 grants for The School of Life Project—Developing Emotional Awareness, http://www.digitalwish.com/dw/digitalwish/product?id=SOLP-001
American Battefield Trust—The Field Trip fund -Civil War Field Trip, https://www.battlefields.org/learn/educators/resources/field-trip-fund

Appendix A

State Farm Good Neighbor Citizenship Company Grants, https://www.statefarm.com/about-us/community-involvement/community-grants/good-neighbor-citizenship-grants

USA TODAY Electronic Edition Grants, http://usatodayeducation.com/k12/usa-today-education-grant-request

Wells Fargo Education Grants, https://www.wellsfargo.com/about/corporate-responsibility/community-giving/

Freeman-McMoran Education Mini Grants, http://www.freeportinmycommunity.com/schools/mini-grants

Nicholas B. Ottaway Foundation K-12 Education Grants, http://www.nbofoundation.org/education-commitee.html

Home Depot Community Impact Grants, https://corporate.homedepot.com/grants/community-impact-grants

The Gilder Lehrman Institute of American History, National History Teacher of the Year https://www.gilderlehrman.org/content/national-history-teacher-year

Appendix B

Canadian Grant Opportunities

Canada Post Community Foundation, https://www.canadapost.ca/web/en/pages/aboutus/communityfoundation/criteria.page
Best Buy School Tech Grants, https://www.bestbuy.ca/en-CA/school-tech-grants.aspx
Air Canada Community Support, https://www.aircanada.com/ca/en/aco/home/about/corporate-responsibility/community.html
Aviva Community Fund, https://www.avivacommunityfund.org
CAAWS (Canadian Assoc. for the Advancement of Women), http://www.caaws.ca/grants-and-recognition/wise-fund/application-process-2/
Community One Foundation Rainbow Grants, http://communityone.ca/grants-awards/
DreamCatcher Fund, http://www.dcfund.ca/index.php?id=sports-recreation
EcoLeague, http://lsf-lst.ca/en/projects/teacher-resources/action-project-funding
Farm Credit Canada (FCC) AgriSpirit Fund, https://www.fcc-fac.ca/en/in-your-community/giving-back/fcc-agrispirit-fund.html
Goodlife Kids Foundation, https://www.goodlifekids.com/the-grant-program/
Greenbelt Fund, http://www.greenbeltfund.ca/applying_for_a_grant
The Honda Canada Foundation, http://www.hondacanadafoundation.ca/apply-for-funding
Hydro One Power Play Grant, https://www.hydroone.com/about/indigenous-relations/power-play
Imperial Oil Charitable Foundation, >http://www.imperialoil.ca/en-ca/community/community-investment
Tree Canada Greening Canada School Grounds Program, https://treecanada.ca/greening-communities/community-tree-grants/
Kids Cops and Computers—Good Citizen Scholarship, http://www.kidscopscomputers.org/students/#grade8
JumpStart-Canadian Tire, http://jumpstart.canadiantire.ca/content/microsites/jumpstart/en/community-accessibility-grants.html

Ken Spencer Award, http://www.cea-ace.ca/webform/ken-spencer-award-application-form

KidSport Ontario, http://www.kidsportcanada.ca/ontario/about-kidsport-ontario/grant-program/

Laidlaw Foundation, http://laidlawfdn.org/funding-opportunities/knowledge-building/

Mountain Equipment Co-op (MEC) Access & Activity Grants, https://www.mec.ca/en/explore/granting

Ontario Active School Travel Fund, https://www.saferoutestoschool.ca/Ontario-active-school-travel-fund/

Ontario Federation of School Athletic Associations (OFSAA) Grade 9 Try Day Program, http://www.ofsaa.on.ca/programs/try-day

Ontario Trillium Foundation, https://otf.ca/what-we-fund?redirected=1

Parents Reaching Out Grants for Regional/Provincial Projects (Ministry of Education), http://www.edu.gov.on.ca/eng/parents/regional.html

Physical Activity in Secondary Schools (PASS) Grant, http://www.edu.gov.on.ca/eng/policyfunding/memos/nov2017/pass_application_en.pdf

President's Choice Nutrition Grant Program, http://www.greenbeltfund.ca/applying_for_a_grant

S'Cool Life Fund, https://www.scoollifefund.ca/index2.php?id=3

Shell Social Investment Grants, https://www.shell.ca/en_ca/sustainability/communities/funding-guidelines-process.html

Speak Up Project, http://www.edu.gov.on.ca/eng/students/speakup/projects.html

TD Friends of the Environment Foundation, https://fef.td.com/funding/

Toyota Evergreen Learning Grounds School Ground Greening Grants, https://www.evergreen.ca/our-projects/school-ground-greening-grants/

WestJet Community Giving, https://www.westjet.com/en-ca/about-us/community-investment/airport-community-giving#tabpane-1474555141004-2

Whole Foods: School Garden Grant, https://www.wholekidsfoundation.org/schools/programs/school-gardens-canada

Youth 4 Action Canadian Cancer Society, http://www.cancer.ca/en/get-involved/take-action/what-you-can-do/youth-4-action-on/?region=on

Go Wild School Grants, http://www.wwf.ca/takeaction/gowildschools/

References

Abramson, P. (2015). 20th annual construction report: National statistics, building trends & detailed analysis. *School Planning & Management*. February, 2015. Retrieved from https://webspm.com/ research/2015/02/annual-school-construction-report/asset.aspx?tc=assetpg&tc=page0&m=1._https://webspm.com/Articles/2015/07/01/School-Costs.aspx; http://citiesandschools.berkeley.edu/uploads/21csf_CC+S_School_Facilities_Cost_Calculator_User_Guide.pdf

Anderson, R. H., & Pavan, B. N. (1993). *Nongradeness: Helping It Happen*. Lancaster, PA: Technomic Publishing Company.

Angell, M. (2011). *The Epidemic of Mental Illness: Why?*. The New York Review of Books. June 23, 2011. Retrieved from https://www.nybooks.com/articles/2011/06/23/epidemic-mental-illness-why/.

Barnes, D. (1976). *From Communication to Curriculum*. Portsmouth, NH: Boynton/Cook-. Heinemann.

Barshay, J. (2016). U.S. now ranks near the bottom among 35 industrialized nations in math. *The Hechinger Report*. December 6, 2016. Retrieved from http://hechingerreport.org/u-s-now-ranks-near-bottom-among-35-industrialized-nations-math/.

Blatchford, P., Moriarty, V., Edmonds, S., & Martin, C. (2002). Relationships between class size and teaching: A multimethod analysis of English infant schools. *American Educational Research Journal, 39*(1), 101–132. Retrieved from http://dx.doi.org/10.3102/00028312039001101.

Blyth Education. Toronto. Retrieved from https://blytheducation.com/blyth-academy/lawrence-park/.

Brooks, J. (2017). From charity towards a social justice paradigm. *LinkedIn*. August 29, 2017. Retrieved from https://www.linkedin.com/pulse/from-charity-towards-social-justice-paradigm-critical-joe-brooks/.

Bryk, A. S., & Driscoll, M. E. (1988). The high school as community: Contextual influences and consequences for students and teachers. National Center on Effective Secondary Schools, Madison, WI. Retrieved from https://eric.ed.gov/?id=ED302539.

Burns, M. (2017). Marilyn Burns Math Blog. March 5, 2017. Retrieved from http://www.marilynburnsmathblog.com/oh-no-99/.

Burt, R. (2014). Forget coding: Let's change up how we teach math!. *The Edublogger.* February 6, 2014. Retrieved from https://www.theedublogger.com/2014/02/06/forget-coding-lets-change-up-how-we-teach-math/.

California Department of Education. (2007). Complete Schools. State Allocation Board Meeting. May 23, 2007. Retrieved from https://www.cde.ca.gov/ls/fa/sf/completesch.asp.

Canada Service Corps. Retrieved from https://www.canada.ca/en/employment-social-development/services/canada-service-corps.html.

Common Core State Standards. (2009). Retrieved from http://www.corestandards.org.

Copp, J., & Smith, B. (2010). *Mining for Gems: A Casebook of Exceptional Practices in Teaching and Learning.* St. Catherines: Canadian Educational Standards Institute.

Croft, A., Coggshall, J. G., Dolan, M., Powers, E., & Killion, J. (2010). Job-embedded professional development: What it is, who is responsible, and how to get it done well. National Comprehensive Center for Teacher Quality. April 2010. Retrieved from https://eric.ed.gov/?id=ED520830.

Curtin, S. C., Warner, M., & Hedegaard, H. (2016). Increase in suicide in the United States, 1999–2014. *NCHS Data Brief.* April 2016 (241), 1–8. Retrieved from https://www.ncbi.nlm.nih.gov/pubmed/27111185.

Darling-Hammond, L. (2005). Teaching as a profession: Lessons in teacher preparation and professional development. *Phi Delta Kappan.* Sage Journals. November 1, 2005. Retrieved from https://doi.org/10.1177/003172170508700318.

DeMoss, K. (2016). For the public good: Quality preparation for every teacher. Bank Street College of Education. June 2016. Retrieved from https://d2mguk73h8xisw.cloudfront.net/media/filer_public/filer_public/2016/06/29/sfp_framework_final_0951.pdf.

Donaldson, M., & Moore Johnson, S. (2011). TFA teachers: How long do they teach? Why do they leave? *Education Week.* October 4, 2011. Retrieved from https://www.edweek.org/ew/articles/2011/10/04/kappan_donaldson.html.

Drake, S. (2012). *Creating Standards Based Integrated Curriculum.* Thousand Oaks, CA: Corwin.

Fisher, D., Frey, N., & Rothenberg, C. (2008). *Content-Area Conversations: How to Plan Discussion-Based Lessons for Diverse Language Learners.* Alexandria: ASCD.

Flanagan, T. (2017). Future school of Fort Smith: A conversation with Trish Flanagan. *Education Reimagined.* November 9, 2017. Retrieved from https://education-reimagined.org/conversation-trish-flanagan/.

Fullan, M., & Langworthy, M. (2014). A Rich Seam: How New Pedagogies Find Deep Learning. *Pearson.* February 22, 2015. Retrieved from https://issuu.com/splinterdesign/docs/pearson_rich_seam.

Gardner, H. (1985). *Frames of Mind: The Theory of Multiple Intelligences.* New York: Basic Books.

Gladden, R. M. (2000). Small schools: What's small? Bank Street Occasional Paper Series. No. 3. Retrieved from https://educate.bankstreet.edu/occasional-paper-series/vol2000/iss3/1/.

Gladwell, M. (2002). *The Tipping Point: How Little Things Can Make a Big Difference*. New York: Little, Brown and Company.

Goldring, R., Taie, S., & Minsun, R. (2014). Teacher attrition and mobility: Results from the 2012–13 teacher follow-up survey: First look. *National Center for Education Statistics*. September, 2014. Retrieved from https://nces.ed.gov/pubs2014/2014077.pdf.

Goodlad, J. I. (1984). *A Place Called School: Prospects for the Future*. New York: McGraw-Hill Book Co.

Grant, J., & Johnson, B. (1994). *A Common Sense Guide to Multi-Age Practices*. Peterborough, NH: Crystal Springs Books.

Grauer, S. R. (2018). Small versus large school: The truth about equity, cost, and diversity of programming in large and small schools. *Community Works Journal*. Community Works Institute. September 19, 2018. Retrieved from https://www.communityworksinstitute.org/cwjonline/essays/a_essaystext/grauer_smallsch1.html.

Grauer, S. R., & Ryan, C. (2018). Small schools: The Myths, reality, and potential of small schools. *Community Works Journal*. Community Works Institute. Retrieved from https://www.communityworksinstitute.org/cwjonline/essays/a_essaystext/grauer_smallschools2.html.

Gutierrez, R., & Slavin, R. E. (1992). Achievement effects of the nongraded elementary school: A best evidence synthesis. *Review of Educational Research*, 62(4), 333–376. EJ 460 525.

Gutsky, T. (2017). Retrieved from https://twitter.com/tguskey/status/955527650977701888.

Hargreaves, A., & Fullan, M. (1996). *What's Worth Fighting for in Schools*. New York: Teacher's College Press.

Habitat for Humanity. Retrieved from https://www.habitat.org.

Howley, C., Strange, M., & Bickel, R. (2000). Research about School Size and School Performance in Impoverished Communities. *ERIC Digest*. Retrieved from https://www.ericdigests.org/2001-3/size.htm.

Husbands, J., & Beese, S. (2004). Review of selected high school reform strategies. *Eric*. Retrieved from https://eric.ed.gov/?id=ED476306.

Hylden, J. (2005). *What's So Big About Small Schools? The Case for Small Schools: Nationwide and in North Dakota*. Boston: Harvard University.

Jemison, M. C. (2016). Planting the Seeds for a Diverse U.S. STEM Pipeline: A Compendium of Best Practice K-12 STEM Education Programs. Updated 2016. Retrieved from https://www.makingsciencemakesense.com/static/documents/Resources/K-12-STEM-edu-programs.pdf.

Katz, L. G., Evangelou, D., & Hartman, J. A. (1990). *The Case for Mixed-Age Grouping in Early Childhood Education*. Washington, DC: National Association for the Education of Young Children. ED 326 302.

Kaffer, N. (2017). How Michigan is failing our teachers. *Detroit Free Press*. May 27, 2017. Retrieved from https://www.freep.com/story/opinion/columnists/nancy-kaffer/2017/05/28/michigan-teacher-shortage/346944001/.

Kamenetz, A. (2017). 4 Things We Don't Know About AP Tests. *nrpEd*. May 1, 2017. Retrieved from https://www.npr.org/sections/ed/2017/05/01/525073237/four-things-we-dont-know-about-ap-tests.

Kubota, T. (2017). Launching the 25th generation of a cutting-edge global teamwork class at Stanford. *Stanford News*. October 25, 2017. Retrieved from https://news.stanford.edu/2017/10/25/launching-25th-generation-cutting-edge-global-teamwork-class-stanford/.

Lave, J., & Wenger, E. (2002). Legitimate peripheral participation in communities of practice. In R. Harrison (Ed.), *Supporting Lifelong Learning: Volume I: Perspectives on Learning* (pp. 111–126). London: Routledge Falmer.

Lee, V. E., Smith, J. B., & Croninger, R. G. (1997). How high school organization influences the equitable distribution of learning in Mathematics and Science. *Sociology of Education*, 70(2), 128–150. April, 1997. Retrieved from https://www.jstor.org/stable/2673160.

Levine, M. (2002). *A Mind at a Time*. New York: Simon & Schuster.

Lodish, R. (1992). The pros and cons of mixed-age grouping. *Principal*, 71(5), 72–74.

Lucas, B., Claxton, G., & Spencer, E. (2013). Progression in student creativity in school: First steps towards new forms of formative assessments, OECD Education Working Papers, No. 86, OECD Publishing. Retrieved from http://dx.doi.org/10.1787/5k4dp59msdwk-en.

Lurie, S. (2013). Why doesn't the constitution guarantee the right to education? *The Atlantic*. October 16, 2013. Retrieved from https://www.theatlantic.com/education/archive/2013/10/why-doesnt-the-constitution-guarantee-the-right-to-education/280583/.

Lynch, M. (2016a). Ineffective assessments, part II: Where assessments stand today. *The Edvocate*. December 28, 2016. Retrieved from http://www.theedadvocate.org/ineffective-assessments-part-ii-assessments-stand-today/.

Lynch, M. (2016b). Ineffective assessments, part III: Why Common Core fails. *The Edvocate*. December 29, 2016. Retrieved from https://www.theedadvocate.org/ineffective-assessments-part-iii-common-core-fails/.

Lynch, M. (2017a). Ineffective assessments, part IV: Greater focus on how to obtain knowledge. *The Edvocate*. January 1, 2017. Retrieved from http://www.theedadvocate.org/ineffective-assessments-part-iv-greater-focus-obtain-knowledge/.

Lynch, M. (2017b). Ineffective assessments, part V: More critical thinking needed. *The Edvocate*. January 2, 2017. Retrieved from http://www.theedadvocate.org/ineffective-assessments-part-v-critical-thinking-needed/.

Lynch, M. (2017c). Ineffective assessments, Part VII: Better cultural and learning understanding. *The Edvocate*. January 4, 2017. Retrieved from http://www.theedadvocate.org/ineffective-assessments-part-vii-better-cultural-learning-understanding/.

Lynch, M. (2017d). *Understanding Key Education Issues: How We Got Here and Where We Go From Here*. Florence: Routledge.

Lynch, M. (2018). Why all assessments should be digital. *The Tech Edvocate*. March 12, 2018. Retrieved from https://www.thetechedvocate.org/why-all-assessments-should-be-digital/.

Mackey, B., Johnson, R. J., & Wood, T. (1995). Cognitive and affective outcomes in a multi-age Language Arts program. *Journal of Research in Childhood Education*, 10(1), 49–61.

Mitra, S. (2012). The Hole in the Wall Project and the power of self-organized learning E-book excerpt. *Edutopia*, George Lucas Educational Foundation. February 3, 2012. Retrieved from https://www.edutopia.org/blog/self-organized-learning-sugata-mitra.

Model United Nations. Retrieved from https://www.nmun.org/about-nmun/mission-and-history.html.

Mojtabai, R., Olfson, M., & Han, B. (2016). National trends in the prevalence and treatment of depression in adolescents and young adults. *Pediatrics*. Retrieved from 10.1542/peds.2016-1878; http://pediatrics.aappublications.org/content/138/6/e20161878.

Moore, T. (2015). This school is using 'Shark Tank' to teach research and presentation skills. *eSchoolNews*. August 25, 2015. Retrieved from https://www.eschoolnews.com/2015/08/25/shark-tank-classroom-249/?ps=smithfamily31@gmail.com-001a000001XiISO-003a00000265XRB.

Nathan, J., & Thao, S. (2001). *Smaller, Safer, Saner Successful Schools*. Washington, DC: National Clearinghouse for Educational Facilities.

National Alliance Public Charter Schools. (2013). Public Charter School facilities: Results from the NAPCS National Charter School Survey, School Year 2011–2012. Retrieved from https://www.publiccharters.org/publications/public-charter-school-facilities-results-napcs-national-charter-school-survey-school-year-2011-2012.

National Council for Teachers of English (NCTE). Retrieved from http://www.readwritethink.org.

Newton, N. (2017). Character for learning and life. *LinkedIn*. October 26, 2017. Retrieved from https://www.linkedin.com/pulse/character-learning-life-dr-nigel-newton/.

OECD. (2012). Equity and Quality in Education: Supporting Disadvantaged Students and Schools. *Spotlight Report*. Netherlands: OECD Publishing. Retrieved from http://www.oecd.org/education/school/49603617.pdf.

OECD. (2015). Education Policy Outlook, Canada. January 2015. Retrieved from http://www.oecd.org/education/EDUCATION%20POLICY%20OUTLOOK%20CANADA.pdf.

Patti, L. (2018). How this UN role playing game helps teachers solve complex challenges together. *EdSurge*. February 12, 2018. Retrieved from https://www.edsurge.com/news/2018-02-12-how-this-un-role-playing-game-helps-teachers-solve-complex-challenges-together.

Pepper, L. (2018). Cool ways to raise cash. *Family Circle*. Retrieved from https://www.familycircle.com/family-fun/volunteering/cool-ways-for-schools-to-raise-cash/.

Perkins, D. (2014). *Future Wise: Educating Our Children for a Future World*. San Francisco: Jossey-Bass.

PHE Canada. Retrieved from http://www.phecanada.ca/programs/physical-literacy.

Pratt, D. (1980). *Curriculum: Design and Development*. New York: Harcourt Brace Jovanovich, Inc.

Raywid, M. A. (1980). Restoring school efficiency by giving parents a choice. *Educational Leadership*. 134–137. November 1980.

Raywid, M. A. (1999). Current literature on small schools. *ERIC Digest*. January 1999. Retrieved from www.ael.org/eric/digests/edoud961.htm.

Rosholm, M., Mikkelsen, M. B., & Gumede, K. (2017). Your move: The effect of chess on mathematics test scores. *PLOS Journal*. May 11, 2017. Retrieved from https://www.ncbi.nlm.nih.gov/pmc/articles/PMC5426665/.

Round Square. Retrieved from https://www.roundsquare.org.

Scardamelia, M., & Bereiter, C. (1994). Computer support for knowledge building communities. *The Journal of the Learning Sciences*, 3(3), 265–283.

Schanzenbach, D. W. (2014). *Does Class Size Matter?* Northwest University: National Educational Policy Center. February 2014. Retrieved from https://nepc.colorado.edu/sites/default/files/pb_-_class_size.pdf.

Schwartz, K. (2014). More progressive ways to measure deeper levels of learning. *Mind/Shift*. April 9, 2014. Retrieved from https://www.kqed.org/mindshift/34821/more-progressive-ways-to-measure-deeper-level-of-learning.

Schwartz, K. (2017a). MIT's Scratch program is evolving for greater, more mobile creativity. *Mind/Shift*. July 17, 2017. Retrieved from https://www.kqed.org/mindshift/48684/mits-scratch-program-is-evolving-for-greater-more-mobile-creativity.

Schwartz, K. (2017b). How to build self-assessment into jampacked high school classes. *Mind/Shift*. November 7, 2017. Retrieved from https://www.kqed.org/mindshift/49222/how-to-build-self-assessment-into-jampacked-high-school-classes.

Schwartz, K. (2017c). How kids benefit from having to explain their math thinking. *Mind/Shift*. March 27, 2017. Retrieved from https://ww2.kqed.org/mindshift/2017/03/27/how-kids-benefit-from-learning-to-explain-math-thinking/.

Sharratt, L., & Harild, G. (2015). *Good to Great to Innovate: Recalculating the Route to Career Readiness, K-12+*. Corwin.

Sizer, T. (2000). Ted Sizer's opening remarks. *Fall Forum 2000*. Providence Rhode Island. December 2, 2009. Retrieved from http://essentialschools.org/horace-issues/ted-sizers-opening-remarks-fall-forum-2000-providence-rhode-island/.

Sky School. Retrieved from https://www.skyschool.world/about-1/.

Slate, J. R., & Jones, C. H. (2005). Effects of School Size: A Review of the Literature with Recommendations. *Essays in Education*, 13, 1–22.

Smith, B. (1994). *Teaching Physical Education: Let Me Count the Ways*. Orbit. Toronto: OISE Press.

Smith, B. (1996) *Inquiry into Peer Teaching*. Doctorate dissertation. Toronto: OISE.

Smith, B. (2016). Charter schools and their revolving doors. *LinkedIn*. November 7, 2016. Retrieved from https://www.linkedin.com/pulse/charter-schools-revolving-doors-barbara-smith/.

Smith, B. (2017). *A Charter School's Principal's Story: A View from the Inside*. Rotterdam: Sense Publishers.

Sornson, B. (2017a). Time for disruptive innovation in our schools. Community Works Institute. January 19, 2017. Retrieved from https://medium.com/communityworksjournal/time-for-disruptive-innovation-in-our-schools-a3e5bb170a25.

Sornson, B. (2017b). Hasn't Worked, Can't Work, Won't Work. Community Works Institute. February 1, 2017. Retrieved from http://blog.communityworksinstitute.org/2017/02/01/hasnt-worked-cant-work-wont-work/.

Stiggins, R. (2008). *Assessment FOR Learning, the Achievement Gap, and Truly Effective Schools*. Portland: ETS Assessment Training Institute. September 8, 2008. Retrieved from https://www.ets.org/Media/Conferences_and_Events/pdf/stiggins.pdf.

Stone, S. J. (1995). Teaching strategies: Strategies for teaching children in multi-age Classrooms. *Childhood Education*, 71(2), 102–105.

Tepylo, D. H., & Floyd, L. (2018). Learning math through coding. *Math + Code 'Zine*. Retrieved in http://researchideas.ca/mc/learning-math-through-coding/.

Uphoff, J. K., & Evans, D. A. (1993). The country school comes to town: A case study of multiage grouping and teaching. In D. Sumner (Ed.), *Multiage Classrooms: The Ungrading of America's Schools. The Multiage Resource Book* (pp. 36–38). Peterborough, NH: Society for Developmental Education.

Villa, R. A., Thousand, J. S., & Stainback, W. (Eds.). (1992). *Restructuring for Caring and Effective Education: An Administrative Guide to Creating Heterogeneous Schools*. Baltimore, MD: P.H. Brookes.

Vygotsky, L. S. (1978). *Mind in Society: The Development of Higher Psychological Processes*. Cambridge, MA: Harvard University Press.

Warne, R. T. (2017). Research on the Academic Benefits of the Advanced Placement Program: Taking Stock and Looking Forward. Sage. Retrieved from http://journals.sagepub.com/doi/full/10.1177/2158244016682996.

Watts, G. D., & Castle, S. (1993). The time dilemma in school restructuring. *Phi Delta Kappan*, 75(4). December 1993. Retrieved from https://www.questia.com/library/journal/1G1-14723499/the-time-dilemma-in-school-restructuring.

Whitby, G. (2018). The big educational spend. *Bluyonder*. July 10, 2018. Retrieved from https://bluyonder.wordpress.com/2018/07/10/the-big-educational-spend/.

Whitehead, J. (2018). *Living Theory Research as a Way of Life*. Bath: Brown Dog Books. Retrieved from https://en.wikipedia.org/wiki/Student activism.

Wooster, M. M. (2018). Charter school funders: Look out for "Turnaround Consultants." *Philanthropy Daily*. July 3, 2018. Retrieved from https://www.philanthropydaily.com/charter-school-funders-look-out-for-turnaround-consultants/.

Yousafzai, M. (2013). *I am Malala: The Story of the Girl Who Stood Up for Education and was Shot by the Taliban*. London: Orion Publishing Group Ltd.

Index

assessment, 49–53; accountability, 8, 14, 50, 52, 100, 131; Advanced Placement (AP), exams, 51, 114; evidence of student learning, 117; mastery, 43, 46, 56, 77, 112, 116, 127; performance review, 72, 115, 132; Program of International Student Assessment (PISA), 51; report card, 102, 116; re-testing, upgrading, 116; standardized tests, 50–52, 116–17, 127; standards, 39, 43, 50, 52, 56

budget, 87–98, 124; administrative costs, 92–93, 95–96, 98, 124; affordability, 129–30; alignment with values, 102, 129–31; consultants, 15, 51, 89, 97, 105; diseconomy of scale, 125; expenditure categories, 87, 93, 107; materiality, 96–98; repurposing existing funds, 96, 123, 125, 130; re-structuring roles, 101–2, 126; saving money, 100–102; staffing, 65–68, 125; sustainability, 92, 96, 98; transparency, 14, 94, 96–98; transportation, 108, 128; volunteers, 102

class size, 55–57, 108, 115–16, 125, 127; condition for learning, 55; Organization for Economic Co-operation and Development (OECD), 119

data, 11; community voices, 120; qualitative data, 11; quantitative data, 11, 118, 130; satisfaction survey, 69, 119; staff and parent voices, 119–20; student voices, 11–20, 109

engaging experiences, 17, 118; boredom, 56; co-curricular, 116; commercial products, 26, 30, 41, 49, 77; creativity and inquiry, 116–17; deep learning and constructivism, 11, 56; electives, 62, 112; enrichment, 116; family products, 111, 117; Fruchters PBL Lab, 30; *Future Scientists Program,* 39; game centre, 110; hands on science, 35; inspired action, 11; learning spaces, 75; legitimate peripheral participation (LPP), 56; makerspaces, 38; making memories, 31; *NASA Space Camp,* 39; peer teaching, 57, 110, 112, 116; *Pi Day,* 42; project based

learning, 29; research study, 112, 116; robotics, 38, 127; *Shark Tank* entrepreneur, 42; solving community problems, 117, 128; stations, 110
English Language Arts (ELA), 29–34; differentiation, 29; E-pals, 30–31; field trips, 116, 127–28; imagination class at *New School*, 110; long term projects, 31; novel writing, 31; reading, 29–30; software/digital resources, 30; textbooks, 30

facilities, 75–79; align with school niche, 117; budget allocation for maintenance, renovations, utilities, 95–96; community values, 108; flexible facility standards, 78–79; *Hole in the Wall Project*, 76; *New School* facility ideas, 108–10; office spaces, 77–78; renovations, 77; safety and security, 129; *School Construction Project*, 128; shared facilities, 79; student work, 77, 110, 117; welcoming, 109
fine arts, 29–34, 111; arts credits outside school, 34; Centre for the Arts at *New School*, 109–10; Dramatic Arts, 33, 110; instrument maintenance, 32; media arts, 33; multiple medium visual artists, 32–33; music, 32

Gardner, Howard, 45
Gladwell, Malcolm, 5
global citizens, 25–28; *Flat Stanley* stories, 26; mapping center, 110; Model United Nations, 25–26; refugees, 25–26; school/community museum, 110; *Sky School,* 25; world languages, 26, 111–12, 120
Goodlad, John, 59
greatness defined, 11, 114–15, 130, 133; beyond "sameness," 85; cost of, 123; funding great schools, 100; goal of *New School*, 107–8; ideal school, 105; transformation, 105

Guskey, Thomas, 107

innovation, 11–12, 115, 119; affordable change, 85; flexible space standards, 79; grant influence, 99–100, 125; innovation funding, 13, 124; missed opportunity in charter schools, 95; outlier ideas, 107, 130; re-organizing and re-chunking of courses, 114; risk, 105; spaces, 77; staff restructuring, 66
intellect, 19, 116

Laban, Rudolf, 46

math, 41–44; chess, value of, 42, 110; coding and patterning, 42–43; digital math resources, 41; math games, 42; resources, 41
money managers, 13–15

parents, 15–16; co-learners, 117, 117; *March of our Lives*, 16
Perkins, David, 17
physical education, 45–48, 111; credits, 46; Daily Quality Physical Education, 46; dance and PE, 46; lifelong physical skills, 46; outdoor education, 46; physical intelligence, 45

reform, 11, 12, 61, 115, 119, 123, 129–30; re-invent the wheel, 5; "sameness," 129

scheduling, 59–64; 4-day week, 127; block scheduling, 60; calendar, 59; consolidation time, 60; co-op course, 114; flexible schedule, 61; internships, 62; intersession/co-curricular options, 61; lopping, 61; Macro Monday elective day, 112; Monday to Friday schedule, 112; multi-age learning, 61; niche of the school, 62–63; reducing subject

load, 60; semester programming, 60; single gender classes, 63, 112, 116; time as resource, 59
school improvement, 1, 12, 17, 67, 120, 121; accountability, 14; budgeting to improve, 85, 87, 94; change and sustainability, 96; driver of change, 103; imitation, 107; implementation, 5; integrated school, 66; new sources of revenue, 99; scarcity, 102; small schools and quality control, 82, 125–26; strategic planning, 121; vertical alignment of K–12 curriculum, 119
science and technology, 35–40, 127
Sizer, Ted, 56
small schools, 81–84; academic benefits, 81; Community Works Institute, 82; enhanced safety, 82; superschools, 82–83, 125
social and emotional learning (SEL), 19–25; 4H Club, 21; belonging and inclusion, 20, 118–19; bullying and cyberbullying, 20; character education, 22, 110, 112, 119; community works class, 109–10, 112, 118; depression, suicide, and resilience, 19; empathy, 19; employability skills, 21, 112; Habitat for Humanity, 21; happiness and fun, 119; health, 20, 110, 112, 119; internships, 21; meditation, 21; mental health, 19–21, 116, 119; *New School* culture, 109; nursing home field trips, 20, 22; *Outward Bound*, 22; pro-social skills, 20, 116; reducing discipline incidents, 21; *Round Square,* 21; service learning, 20, 110, 112, 119
staff development, 67–74; action research, 72–73; budget Proportion for PD, 95, 97; Chalk Talks at New *School*, 115; examination of student work, 67; *Harvard Project Zero*, 70; surveys, 67; mentoring, 69, 115, 117, 125; *New School* budget, 127; off-site conferences, 70; performance review, 115; professional development days, 115; professional memberships, 31, 41, 36, 45, 117; teacher leadership, 71–72, 117, 125–26; teachers as conference presenters, 71, 127; teachers as curriculum writers and reviewers, 74, 115, 119; teaching principal, 72; team planning and teaching, 70, 11, 115

trustees, 15

unions, 13, 21
university influence and affiliation, 15, 117

Vygotsky, Lev, 56

Whitehead, Jack, 72

Yousafzai, Malala, 121